WHEN YOUR WORLD FALLS APART

Life Lessons from a Ground Zero Chaplain

MIKE MACINTOSH

Run So That You May Win
ivictor.com

Victor is an imprint of
Cook Communications Ministries, Colorado Springs, Colorado 80918
Cook Communications, Paris, Ontario
Kingsway Communications, Eastbourne, England

WHEN YOUR WORLD FALLS APART
© 2002 by Mike MacIntosh

First Printing, 2002
Printed in the United States of America

1 2 3 4 5 6 7 8 9 10 Printing/Year 05 04 03 02

Editors: William J. Kritlow, John Conaway
Cover Design: Image Studios

Unless otherwise noted, Scripture quotations are taken from *The Holy Bible: New King James Version®*. Copyright © 1979, 1980, 1982 by Thomas Nelson, Inc. All rights reserved. Used by permission.

Library of Congress Cataloging-in-Publication Data

CIP data applied for.

ISBN 0-7814-3889-6

CONTENTS

FOREWORD

What can I say? I love Mike MacIntosh! I have never met anyone with a greater compassion for those who don't know Christ, or a more generous spirit towards those who do. His entire church body is permeated with his attitude of Christ-like love.

I met Mike for the first time about ten years ago when he and his wife, Sandy, took me to dinner before I spoke at his church. We had no sooner been seated in the restaurant than one of the waiters came over to confirm Mike's identity—then said shyly that he had given his life to Jesus Christ as a result of hearing Mike preach. Mike's response to him was so attentively loving, it was as though he had nothing to do but give his time to one who was basically interrupting our dinner. And I praised God for the glimpse into Mike's heart that the incident gave me.

The next time I was in San Diego, as the bellboy was taking my luggage to my hotel room, I began to share the Gospel with him. He grinned, then gave me his testimony. He had been down and out on drugs when he had heard the Gospel. He responded to the message by repenting of his sin and giving his heart to Christ. When I inquired who the preacher was, he replied, "Mike MacIntosh." And again, I praised God for Mike's impulsive compulsion to share Jesus.

But Mike not only shares Jesus with the lost, he has a beautiful gift of building up those who are in the family of faith. Because we live on separate coasts, I rarely see Mike and Sandy in person. But occasionally, when I open my email, I have a note of exhortation and encouragement from Mike. Sometimes he has been prompted to write by something he has seen about me in the national media, sometimes it has been prompted by his awareness of my speaking schedule, sometimes there seems to be no reason at all— except that each time he has conveyed in his funny style of misspelled, grammatically incorrect words a message straight from God to my heart. Again and again, with tears rolling down my cheeks, I have read his emails and wondered how in the world he knew the discouragement I was feeling, or the temptation I was facing, or the confirmation I so desperately needed. In so many ways, Mike has been the pastor to me that I have not had since childhood.

And so with great eagerness I awaited the arrival of his manuscript, *When Your World Falls Apart*. As I have read it, my heart has been touched, thrilled, moved, challenged, and blessed by every page. Like his personal emails to me, this book contains insights and wisdom, encouragement and exhortation that will leave you wondering, "How did Mike MacIntosh know . . . ?" And like me, you will come to the conclusion, "It must be the Lord!"

If you have gone through Ground Zero—not in lower Manhattan, but in your own experience—or if you know of someone who is there now, I heartily recommend this book to you.

Anne Graham Lotz

PREFACE

Mere words will never be able to explain what happened on September 11, 2001 at the World Trade Center in New York City. Millions of words will be written from just as many points of view. Yet the devastation that occurred was not only of the physical Twin Towers themselves and the surrounding real estate; we must also take into account the human lives that were lost, and the impact those losses continue to have on the lives of families, friends, and loved ones.

Yet if the impact of 9/11 were to end there, the world would still have a gaping hole in its heart that probably could never be healed. But it didn't stop there; the destruction has also had a profound effect on the lives of all the emergency personnel, rescue workers, construction workers, the New York Police Department, Fire Department New York, New York Port Authority, and the myriad of other agencies involved in the investigation and rescue and recovery efforts at Ground Zero.

It is to the surviving family, friends, loved ones and response personnel that I humbly dedicate this book. A few thousand words that will not long be remembered nor quoted; nevertheless, this book is an attempt to expedite healing with a cup of cold water and the love of God.

When I was asked to write this book I didn't anticipate the amount of pain I would feel as I typed. The smells and sounds of Ground Zero became very alive to me once again. The faces of the tired rescue workers were recalled as my mind wandered through my memories. The tired and weary workers at the morgue and our many conversations were once again in my thought patterns. I could hear the voices and sounds in the Family Assistance Center as if I were standing there live. Twice while writing I had to stop and cry because my heart was hurting as the past became the present one more time.

However, my own pain reminds me that this is why I have written this book. I know that the suffering of so many people needs to be brought to a closure. If one person can read these words and say, "It is finished," then it has been worth the effort. My prayer is that this book will be used to help you and to direct you from your present position in life to one of joy and happiness.

Though this book contains stories from Ground Zero, it is not a book about Ground Zero; it is a book for everyone who experiences Ground Zeros in their own lives. I trust you will find within this book the words of hope and encouragement you need, and that God will use these words to lead you to higher ground and a peace that passes all understanding.

I thank God for the opportunity to serve as one of the hundreds of chaplains at Ground Zero. God enabled us, and thousands of volunteers, to help those who were suffering in the wake of 9/11. As you prayerfully read these pages, may you find the tender touch of God for the Ground Zeros in your own life.

San Diego, California
April, 2002

You are not reading this book by accident. This book has been placed in your hands for a purpose. Though this book deals with some events in the aftermath of the collapse of the World Trade Center, it is written for people who are facing or have faced their own personal Ground Zeros. We have all faced them, or probably will face them again in our lives. Sometimes events enter into our lives that are as devastating to us as the events in New York City were to millions of people. To the parents of a runaway child, the mother who has lost her son, the businessperson who's had to file bankruptcy, their issues are Ground Zeros.

WHEN YOU'RE AT GROUND ZERO

When your world collapses it doesn't usually happen in an instant. It's usually caused by a series of events. Maybe just one event triggered the collapse, but usually there are many factors that led to that major event. A divorce doesn't happen in one day; it often takes struggling couples years to come to the end of their ability to stay married. Post-abortion stress may take a long time to develop; when it does, it becomes a Ground Zero. I prayed last night with a minister whose son was just convicted of a crime and sentenced to three years in prison. His tears and broken heart reveal to the world that he has a Ground Zero situation before him.

Ground Zero situations vary in magnitude and scope. What may mean a collapsing world to one person may just be a large problem to somebody else. But both people need to be assured that this will pass and that peace will finally come.

On September 11, 2001, a major event was recorded in the annals of history. The terrorist destruction of the twin towers of the World Trade Center shook the world. The death toll has been and will continue to be a nightmare for tens of thousands of people. Unfortunately for many of these people, the nightmare will never go away. I hope and pray that God's love will somehow bring peace to the troubled hearts and minds of these people.

In this book I wish to point the direction to the way out of the darkness that surrounds a collapsing world. Often people feel like the light at the end of the tunnel is nothing more than an oncoming train. When people in crisis don't feel like there is real light at the end of the tunnel, they lose hope; and in losing hope for a closure they lose direction for their lives. If you were to look around you today in your circle of influence, you might be surprised to see the number of people who have lost direction for living. It is a sad fact of our fast-paced society that so many people are lost and lonely. If you were to take a day and focus on the people in your school or office or neighborhood, maybe even your own family, you would see that there are a lot of Ground Zeros close to you.

THE MAKING OF A GROUND ZERO CHAPLAIN

Through a lifetime of experience and training, God prepared me for ministry—not only at Ground Zero in New York, but in the lives of thousands of people who have had to face their own Ground Zeros. For over thirteen years I have served as a police chaplain, and for six years before that as a reserve police officer. I have been trained and certified in Critical Incident Stress Management and am a certified teacher for Critical Incident Law Enforcement Enhancement. I am a member of the Police Officer Standards and Training curricula committee for certification for law enforcement chaplains for the State of California. I have earned three Master Degrees, one of which specialized in chaplain work, as well as a Doctor of Ministry degree. My education and experience in posttraumatic stress syndrome and critical incident counseling and debriefing has enabled me to reach out to people in tragic times of need.

At the writing of this book I have been a pastor for 28 years in San Diego. What started as a home Bible study with ten people has become a congregation of several thousand people—people who not only enjoy worshiping God, but also enjoy serving Him by serving people in the world around them. In fact, from the day after Christmas in 2001 until the end of March 2002 we had a team of 11 people leave San Diego every week to serve at the respite center at Ground Zero in New York City. Today, there are close to 100 churches and affiliate ministries throughout San Diego County, the United States, and around the globe that have grown out of this ministry.

These credentials provide opportunities for me to minister; they don't energize or empower that ministry.The compassion of God has affected my life with a zeal and desire to make a positive impact on the lives of people who need and want help and love. It is not my background or experience that touches people or helps people; it is God's Holy Spirit, who lives in me and directs me to the people He wants to love and help. I have come to love people in a way that can only be attributed to God's love, and my greatest joy is to see people develop into servants who also show God's love to others.

Because of my law enforcement background, education, and experience, I was invited to be part of a spiritual care team that would respond to national air disasters. In the event of an aircraft disaster, a team of chaplains is dispatched to the scene to begin helping the families of victims and survivors. For every victim of an airplane crash, there are about ten people who come to the scene of the crash. In the case of the Egypt Air crash on the East Coast of the United States a few years ago, there were 250 passengers—but about 2500 people related to them came, suffering and hurting, to find out what they could. Funeral services were arranged, and counseling services were handled. When the first airplane crashed into the Twin Towers, my team was activated. That is how I arrived on the scene that is going to be described to you in the following chapters.

THE PURPOSE OF THIS BOOK

This book has been arranged with a specific purpose in mind: to help bring closure to your own Ground Zero. If your world is falling apart, I want to help you withstand the devastation and the blow to your life. I want to offer you help and a shoulder to cry on. The book has been divided into four sections. These four sections are actually the four phases of a disaster, and each chapter within each section is designed to move you along emotionally to the next.

As you progress in the book, it is my hope that your heart will start healing. This is not a medical book, nor is it a mental health book. It is not a quick fix or cure-all. You will not read about "ten easy steps to healing" or some sugar-coated words to make you feel good about yourself. But what you will read are true words written from a heart of love and concern for you. You will find words of hope and encouragement directed to helping you out of the pain and emotional trauma you might find yourself in. It is filled with eternal words from the world's best-selling book—the Bible—timeless words that have proven to meet the deepest needs of the heart. My prayer is that you will find words that will speak especially to your need, words that will leap off the written page into your heart.

When I was younger, before I was ever a friend of God, I lost my wife and children. I lost my sanity and my mind. I lost direction in life and I lost hope. Though I was a lost young man, one day while wandering aimlessly I found a great treasure. I can identify with Jesus' parable in Matthew 13:44. In this parable, a man found a treasure in a field, so he sold everything he had and bought the field so he could claim the treasure. You see, I found God as the treasure. God gave me my wife and children back, and He gave me my sanity and mind back, and now I want to share that treasure with you.

THE FOUR STAGES

This will be the path the book will take you on as you begin reading each chapter.

The first stage of an event is the disaster itself. With the disaster comes shock and disbelief. All of us experienced this shock when we viewed all the replays over and over again of the commercial jetliners crashing into the World Trade Center. When we go through our own Ground Zeros, we experience a similar shock and disbelief. And those emotions affect every area of our life.

The second stage of a critical incident is the rescue effort. The rescue effort marks an emotional shift for the people involved; it becomes a time of hope. During this stage, the workers at Ground Zero were climbing around the rubble looking for people who were trapped and alive. They kept going because of the hope that someone was going to make it out alive. In our personal Ground Zeros the same is true. Once the shock of the bankruptcy decision is over or the shock that you have been served divorce papers has subsided, then you try to rescue everything you can. Thinking that counseling or talking things out will save the situation, you have hope.

The third stage is an uncomfortable one. This is the recovery effort. The recovery effort takes place once it becomes obvious that no one is left alive; the rescue workers try to recover the remains of the deceased. You probably remember New York Mayor Giuliani sadly telling the public on television that the rescue efforts were ended and the recovery effort was starting. This same shift takes place in your collapsing world too. You begin to realize the facts, they stare you right in the face, and you understand things can never be the same. You know for sure life will never be like it used to be before this event entered your life. You then begin to do your best to recover from the pain, suffering, and emotional trauma of your Ground Zero.

The fourth and final stage is the closure period. Many times we find that this part of a major incident is very difficult. Guilt can plague you, and your emotions can be in turmoil, preventing you from making the decision to move forward with your life. In this portion of the book you'll be encouraged to turn your eyes to God and let Him lead you to a place of healing. Closure is a must; otherwise you will spend the rest of your life wandering in a gloomy world of sadness and indecision. Jesus Christ has a different design for your life: "I have come that they may have life, and have it to the full" (John 10:10).

Each section contains several chapters dealing with the issues you will face in that stage of your Ground Zero. Each chapter has one or more true stories from my firsthand experience at Ground Zero in New York City. Then I've added related anecdotes and relevant Scriptures to help you each step of the way on your journey toward healing and happiness.

May God bless you as you read on, and may His Holy Spirit bring love to you as you have never known before. Be patient with yourself as you grow stronger every day. And trust in God's great wisdom that He will use the Ground Zero situations of your life to draw you closer to Him.

SECTION I:
DISASTER

CHAPTER 1
MAKE OR BREAK?

*But may the God of all grace, who called us to His eternal glory by
Christ Jesus, after you have suffered a while, perfect, establish, strengthen,
and settle you.*

1 Peter 5:10

The air was filled with the noxious smell of death. It was near midnight, and the New York streets that once glowed with streetlights and light from adjacent office buildings were canyons of darkness with no street lamps and office building windows black and vacant. Once inside the barricades and past the security checkpoints, even first-time visitors know they are about to encounter something monstrously unpleasant.

It was only a few days after two planes tore into the twin towers of the World Trade Center. Several blocks from Ground Zero, we could see the sun-brilliant lights of the emergency systems. They lit an area of devastation that, these many months later, I'm still not fully able to comprehend. I am not sure the human mind was ever designed to absorb, to totally grasp, destruction like this. Mounds of twisted, angry rubble, acres of it, burning and hissing at so many levels, with fire hoses hammering it with rivers of water trying to cool the steel girders and debris, while hundreds of Fire Department New York (FDNY) personnel climbed over the pile in a desperate search for survivors.

WHEN WALLS FALL DOWN

It was still called a *rescue effort*. In a matter of days it would reluctantly turn to *recovery*, but for now, they still hoped to find people alive somewhere in the rubble. But regardless of what they called it, every second that ticked by, the men and women who responded to this disaster would have their lives changed forever.

The fire and water produced a mix of steam and smoke that clouded the New York air for miles around, and with those brilliant lights shining through it, it brought to those canyons of darkness a sense of eeriness, a haunting surrealism. NYPD detective Carlos Aviles and I were walking down one of those canyons and were still a couple blocks from the scene when we saw two firemen coming towards us. With that ghostly light still behind them, they were only dark silhouettes, but even so, we could see that they walked with deliberate, plodding steps—as if in shock, as if they were soldiers emerging from a war zone. As we drew closer, we saw that their stern, stoic faces were streaked gray with dirt and sweat. We heard their deep coughs as they hacked and spit the hours of dust and death from their lungs. Their heavy jackets were thrown over their shoulders and their protective helmets, looking like nothing on earth could dislodge them, covered their heads displaying FDNY, their battered but proud badge of honor. They would stop now and again and press the respirator air mask to their faces and breathe deeply, seeking any relief they could find. To me, at least, it looked like no two men on this earth deserved rest more.

Yet none of this scene was new. I'd seen it so many times before.

However, our brief conversation with them was something new and unusual.

We walked up to them and I said, as I had to so many others, "Just want to let you know how much we appreciate what you're doing. How are you guys holding up?"

And for the next few minutes we shuffled the usual stack of words and phrases back and forth, men trying to remain men in the face of the overwhelming. But then one of them, the bigger of the two, maybe six-one, 230 pounds, stopped, his face lost what little edge it had been able to maintain, and he said, "You know, I was molested as a boy. And I've been an alcoholic most of my life. I've been off the booze now for about fourteen months."

A little taken aback by the confession, I managed, "I'm pleased to hear that part of it."

His partner, seeing the conversation beginning to go where he didn't want it to go, said, "Well, I got problems too, but I'll talk about 'em later," and he turned, and I saw his eyes fill with tears. At that moment his cell phone rang and he took the opportunity to bury his pain in that call.

The first firefighter went on, "My life's a real mess. I gotta talk."

And so we did.

YOUR GROUND ZERO

I've been in the ministry thirty-two years and have done a lot of counseling. It generally takes some time for someone to trust a counselor enough to reveal something that personal, that devastating about their past, yet this man opened up to us within less than ten minutes.

For that firefighter (and probably for thousands, maybe even millions of others) the tortured chaos of Ground Zero and the way it occurred—quickly, stealthily, taking the everyday and making it a sinister weapon against us—touched and exposed a "Ground Zero" in his own life. That time when his foundations were shaken, when the world around him crumbled, when those elements of his life he held dear and saw as his protection from evil turned against him and became the very thing they were to protect him from. God was at work within that dear man. How He worked remains between the two of them, but *that* He worked affirmed a great hope within me.

All of us experience Ground Zeros in our lives, great losses that shake our foundations, our lives, our faith—loss of career, loved ones, marriages, children, grandchildren—times in our lives when we are overwhelmed by tragedy or just the sheer magnitude of events, when we feel helpless and it seems that the great towers of our lives are about to crumble into a heap of ruin, crushing us beneath them.

While at Ground Zero I saw countless people dealing with all elements of that horrific attack just as, in my pastoral ministry, I've seen so many dear people deal with the Ground Zeros they've encountered. And I've come to know that just as 9/11/01 was a watershed moment for our country, other Ground Zero events are watersheds in the lives of God's people. They can either *make* or *break* a life.

I don't mean to be trite at this moment. My point is serious. Remember the nursery rhyme "Humpty Dumpty"? Sure you do. We've all learned it from diaper days.

> *Humpty Dumpty sat on a wall,*
> *Humpty Dumpty had a great fall.*
> *All the king's horses and all the king's men,*
> *Couldn't put Humpty Dumpty together again.*

What is this poem really saying? No matter how cheerfully we say it, no matter how much fun we're having, it's telling us that when we fall, when we hit Ground Zero (just as good ol' Humpty did), our fate is to just lie there in pieces. Nobody—not the king, not anyone—can help. The remainder of our lives will remain broken, disjointed—and hope is gone.

I want to lovingly assure you that hope is possible. And my purpose in writing this book is to tell you, show you, and help you experience why. I want to proclaim to you that the pieces can be put back together again, and often in such a way as to build a life that's stronger, more meaningful, more exciting and abundant than the one you knew before.

As the pages turn, I hope to relate what I saw and experienced at Ground Zero and apply those insights to your personal journey of reconstruction and renewal. In the next chapter we'll take a look at the site of the rubble from the Twin Towers, and relate it to how your own Ground Zero might look.

BEND OR BREAK?

My pastor, Chuck Smith, has many words of wisdom that fit everyday living. One of the sayings of his is appropriate for this situation: "Blessed are the flexible, for they shall not be broken."

You see, Ground Zero is either going to make or break that FDNY fireman. When situations become overwhelming to us it is very natural to try to hide the pain. We want to escape the reality of the situation. This is where alcohol and drug abuse come into play. We have found in recent years there is a new opiate for the masses. It is more insidious than previous self-destructive addictions. It is called pornography. We've discovered that people with this addiction are often harder to cure than people with a heroin problem.

Yes, it is true. You can face the situation at hand or you can run from it.

Though it is painful to truthfully accept the facts and deal with the trauma, this situation can make you into a stronger person. This situation can *make you* become a more understanding, loving, and compassionate person. Or you can take the shortcuts to cover up your pain and discomfort and the situation will ultimately *break you*. If you deny the reality of your Ground Zero, the years of pain and suffering will break your spirit in the long run. No matter what you use to cover up your hurt, the situation will still be there in the morning when you wake up.

The Bible says, "God is love." And since He is a God of love, He wants you to live a fruitful, abundant life. He can reach into your heart and help you with the healing you need. Peter was an interesting character. He made so many mistakes in his earlier years while following Jesus. One time he reproved Jesus for saying that He would go to Jerusalem and suffer. Another time he said: "Even if all fall away on account of you, I never will." Jesus answered him, "I tell you the truth . . . this very night, before the rooster crows, you will disown me three times" (Matt. 26:33-34). Sure enough, Peter was confronted three times by people at the judgment of Jesus, and he denied that he knew Him or that he was one of His disciples. And on the third denial the rooster crowed announcing a brand new day. Jesus just turned and looked at Peter. Needless to say, Peter was very distraught. If that were the end of the story we would have no hope today. When Jesus was resurrected from the tomb He met Mary Magdalene in the garden. And He gave her a message: to go and tell the disciples and *Peter* that He had risen from the dead and that He would meet them in Galilee. Thank God He said "and Peter"! You see, He did not want the disciples to mistrust Peter or put him out of their company. He loved Peter, just as He loves you. And He knew that Peter was hurting and probably down on himself. He wanted Peter to be healed and to become mature in his painful situation.

As you read Peter's writings you quickly realize that God's love healed him of his impetuous manner and of his own self-reliance. You can see by his own words that God's grace brought him healing and comfort.

But may the God of all grace, who called us to His eternal glory by Christ Jesus, after you have suffered a while, perfect, establish, strengthen, and settle you. (1 Peter 5:10)

Peter's experience made him an authority on suffering. He was arrested for preaching the resurrection message, and he was crucified on a cross. He did not feel worthy to be executed in the same manner as his Lord, so he asked to be hung upside down. Yes, Peter knew pain and suffering, and his words can bring hope and comfort to you today. Note that he said, "after you have suffered a little while." It may be hard to believe, but your Ground Zero is for "a little while." But it will pass. When it has passed, will it make you or break you? You get to choose. It is your life and your decision. Peter decided to let his Ground Zeros make him a better man.

You can see it in his own words. God will "restore you and make you strong, firm and steadfast." You must be patient with yourself during these times. And hold on to God's promise.

CHAPTER 2
BITTER OR BETTER?

Trust in the Lord with all your heart,
And lean not on your own understanding;
In all your ways acknowledge Him,
And He shall direct your paths.

Proverbs 3:5-6

My beeper chirped. After the moment it took to figure out what it was, I crawled out of my hotel bed and stumbled across the room to where I'd laid it the night before. It was 6:41 A.M. and the beeper flashed a Washington, D.C. phone number. I was in Los Angeles and in a couple hours was to speak at a pastor's conference.

I am a member of a National Disaster Response Team. My job as a law-enforcement chaplain is to provide spiritual care to those touched by an airline tragedy. Eight chaplains are on call every month, and the only time I wear that beeper is when I am on call. September, 2001, was my month.

I called the number and was told by the communication center in Washington, D.C. that less than an hour before a commercial airliner had crashed into one of the twin towers of New York's World Trade Center. Our team was being activated. Although that same voice told me I had four hours to catch a flight from San Diego (where my home is), I took an anxious second to flip on the television so I could get caught up on the latest news.

When we were in training, we were told that for every person taken in an airline disaster, ten other people—family and friends, ten whose lives would never be the same—come to the scene. The 1999 *Egypt Air* crash bore this out. Two hundred-fifty passengers were on board, and nearly 2,500 other souls arrived—all of them distraught, all seeking answers, all in need of spiritual and mental-health professionals to comfort and counsel them.

As I watched this new tragedy unfold, media speculation estimated the death toll in the tens of thousands. I knew I was about to enter a zone of misery and mourning greater than any I could have even contemplated.

God, I whispered, flipping the television off, *be there with me. And help all of the the suffering families and friends.*

WHEN DISASTER STRIKES

There is a moment when you know your Ground Zero has struck. Perhaps you're told in a phone call, maybe one that wakes you in the middle of the night from a sound sleep. Perhaps you know the moment you realize you're in a hospital bed regaining consciousness. Maybe the realization comes on slowly, little by little. Maybe you're not even aware there's a problem until it's too late. It doesn't matter when or how you know, what matters is *that* you know. And *what* you know is that your world has come apart, your foundations have crumbled, and everything familiar has changed. Your world, and perhaps your faith, are shaken. Thousands of people who had loved ones working at the World Trade Center that morning discovered—through the media or phone calls from friends, some even through phone calls from loved ones who were about to die—that their Ground Zero had struck. Their worlds had crashed down. What do you do at that horrific moment?

TRAGEDY'S TRIANGLE

While making my way through Los Angeles rush-hour traffic, listening to the local newsradio station, I learned that the second plane had struck. My cell phone rang, and it was Washington. The incident was now officially dubbed a terrorist attack. In my mind, the number of souls that had been suddenly thrust into a public and private torment had doubled.

Wisely, the United States government immediately grounded all aircraft, commercial and private. As a private pilot who's flown for years, I knew this action probably saved even more lives. We will probably never know exactly how many airplanes had been targeted that day. But even though it was a wise decision, the grounding delayed me. A trip that normally took five hours took three days. But after flying from Los Angeles to Philadelphia, renting a car in Philadelphia, and driving the rest of the way, I finally arrived in New York.

Before we go on, let me describe the arena where I ministered. Picture it as a triangle. At the top, put the actual Ground Zero, the tangled pile of devastation where the Twin Towers had stood. Hopefully I'll find some words to describe that scene later. At the bottom right is the Family Assistance Center, which was open from 8 a.m. to midnight. For the first week, it was set up in the National Guard Armory—an old, much-used building with large front doors and scores of cheap folding tables and chairs inside. Behind those tables were hundreds of public servants, each skating on the knife-edge of emotional breakdown, all but overwhelmed by what they were being asked to do: to carry the news of life or death to the thousands of anguished, frightened people who lined up day and night in front of those tables waiting for news about those they loved. On the left corner of the triangle is the morgue, the Medical Examiner's facilities. This building had yellow tents set up outside to handle the remains of victims from Ground Zero and hundreds of workers clad in those dull green scrubs. Refrigeration trailers sat beside the building—trailers containing bodies and remains removed from the rubble.

I worked for two weeks in those three places. The hours were long; I usually chose to work sixteen to twenty hours a day—a twelve-hour day was a luxury. I was to provide spiritual care to anyone who needed it and to place spiritual-care personnel where they were needed to cover all shifts in all three areas. What qualified me to be there? Over the previous nineteen years I had accumulated critical-incident training and law-enforcement experience and had been involved in crisis-intervention counseling. I'd also been a pastor and counselor for thirty-one years and had related graduate degrees. But for all that experience and all that training, all those hours in the classroom and the field, as I stepped into that triangle of tragedy I couldn't see how any of it prepared me for what I was about to encounter.

AT THE MORGUE

As you read this book, you'll come to see that dealing with tragedy, although difficult and emotional, is a process and must be taken a step at a time. In this book I'll describe some experiences that illustrate that process. As I look back on what happened I can link many of those experiences to the stages I've observed people go through in my critical-incident counseling and debriefings.

When I arrived I went to work at the Family Assistance Center first. But the following experience, which illustrates an early part of the process, took place a couple days later at the morgue. The New York Medical Examiner's office is about two miles or so from Ground Zero. Access was tightly monitored. To pass through the surrounding barricades, I had to wear a special white plastic ID pass around my neck. Even though it had encryption and holographic properties, the words on it said it all: *Fatality Team.*

In this grim environment, hundreds of men and women toiled around the clock. Their job was to receive, tag, store, and identify thousands upon thousands of grisly remains. It was a massive job. Clerical staffs assisted detectives, who assisted doctors, morticians, and forensic technicians. Within a two-block area ringing the perimeter, police officers by the hundreds stood guard. Though unspoken, the pressure gnawed at everyone. No one wanted to delay any information getting to the families—those tens of thousands who waited with tender, frightened hearts at the Family Assistance Center.

DNA testing was imperative. But that just made the job bigger, far bigger than any mortician team had ever handled before. Even the on-site National Disaster Mortician (DMORT) teams were rapidly overwhelmed. But for all the pressure, all the activity, all the exhaustion, all treated the dead with true dignity. These were the remains of fallen countrymen, and they deserved reverent respect. The sense of dignity and respect was very powerful at this scene; it was awesome for me to experience the dignity and respect shown by everyone involved.

Refrigerated trailers sat on either side of the medical tents. The first day there I noticed two, their air conditioners humming. Three days later there were dozens more. On my first visit, when the folks in charge gave me an orientation, something hit my insides—something I learned had hit everyone involved there at least once. It happened when I first saw a gurney that was inside one of the tents. This was an area where the specialists examined remains. My stomach knotted, became nauseous, and for just a moment I thought I was going to lose it. Curiously enough, it wasn't the morgue or all the death that did that to me, it was the sudden awareness of *why* those gurneys were there—to carry the horrific results of a human tragedy committed by inhuman people.

Although these doctors, morticians, and technicians dealt with death every day and were no strangers to grief and suffering, the magnitude of the effort soon exhausted them physically and drained them emotionally. Although no one denied that the families of the victims needed whatever support we could give, it didn't take a special gift to realize the morgue workers were in desperate need of love and encouragement as well.

Police forensic specialists were also at work. Clad in those same dull green scrubs instead of their sharply creased class A blues, their job was to investigate this crime of all crimes. Although they were generally upbeat, the job was beginning to take its toll on them, too. One of them (let's call her Maria) an attractive, petite policewoman, made a lasting impression on me.

ROOTS OF BITTERNESS

I met Maria one evening when I was at the morgue, moving from place to place, encouraging where I could. I stopped to speak with her. She was personable and talkative. I quickly found out she was born in Puerto Rico, and was the single mother of three small girls. She really didn't look like she made a living arresting bad guys. Instead, she was striking enough to land on the cover of a leading women's magazine to model designer clothes. Although she looked twenty-five, she was nearly forty, and had been with the NYPD for nineteen years. It didn't take long to tell that Maria was one sharp cop. She felt comfortable because I was a law enforcement chaplain, so she kept talking.

And I gladly listened.

We sat on a bench across from the examination tables. For whatever reason, she'd let me into her world and spoke to me as a friend. And as she did, she ended up facing some pretty tough issues.

As with the firefighter in the previous chapter, the Ground Zero effect had done its work in Maria's heart. I was a perfect stranger, but that didn't matter. I was willing to listen. As we sat there, our elbows on our knees, her emotional wounds, some long buried but still festering, began to release their toxic poisons. A year or so earlier, her husband had left her and the kids for another woman. He'd left them to pretty much fend for themselves. And Maria just couldn't make it. She worked such long, exhausting hours, but no matter how much overtime she amassed, there was never enough money. And since she was always working, there was never enough time to be with the children.

The more she spoke, the more animated and heated and angry she became. But Maria was more than angry—she was bitter. I could see it in the hardness of her dark eyes, the sharp downturned cut of her mouth. Bitter about her failed marriage, about how the "bum" had treated her, about how he hardly ever spent time with the kids, but when he did he gave them gifts she couldn't possibly afford. Bitter about her finances, or lack of them. No matter how hard she worked, she never got anywhere. And bitter about this terrorist attack that was sending shock waves through her life.

Bitterness is a pall that hangs over the heart, a shroud woven together with threads of anger, betrayal, helplessness, and hopelessness. Sitting on that bench I saw all four in my new friend Maria. She was profoundly angry with her husband for the injustice he'd visited on her. She felt betrayed. After all, he'd promised before God to be with her till death. She'd counted on him, had children by him, planned her life with him at the center of it—lover, helpmate, provider. And he'd reneged, split. She felt helpless, unable to change any of it. He'd thrust her into a rut with sides so high there was no way to steer out of it. Her future, as she saw it, was hopeless. She was stuck, and her only course of action was to take the beating and hope that over time the scar tissue would build up and dull the pain. That pall fell over her heart and she became bitter.

How about you? Perhaps your story's not too different from my new friend's. Or maybe it's completely different, but the effects are the same—anger, a sense of betrayal, helplessness, and hopelessness—bitterness. But as bad as bitterness is, we could probably live with it if we could contain it, sweep it into one of life's small corners, then get on with enjoying the rest of it. But we can't contain it. Bitterness might start out as a little blemish on an otherwise joyous life, but it grows and hardens. It sends out tendrils and roots that touch, then influence, then strangle other parts of our lives. Bitterness toward her husband tainted Maria's relationship with her daughters, tainted her work life, undoubtedly tainted her days off, holidays, vacations. Even her time with friends, certainly her male friends, was soured. Bitterness hardened her heart and sapped her joy.

Bitterness will do the same to you. And it will for as long as you let it have a foothold. I know a man who blames his father for reneging on an agreement to pay for his college education. Never mind that his father had suffered financial reversals and couldn't come through as planned—this man hasn't spoken to his father in nearly twenty years because, without a college background, he's found it difficult to advance. Bitterness, if held on to, will do far more damage to you than what you're bitter about. The Bible warns us to beware "lest any root of bitterness springing up cause trouble" (Heb. 12:15). Our bitterness sends out roots, and other people are affected.

INSTEAD OF BITTERNESS, BETTERNESS

If you see those roots of bitterness growing in you, what can you do? Let's go back to that bench just outside the morgue and hear what I shared with my dear friend.

After a few minutes I gently interrupted. I told her God wanted to help her, and that He alone could make things work in her life. He would provide for her and help raise her girls, give her the strength at work, wisdom with her finances, and those parental smarts she needed to unravel the knots only kids can tie.

She didn't answer, at first. Instead, she began to cry. The tangle of emotion her morgue work had stirred up trickled down her cheeks. But just as quickly, the trickle was sniffled and wiped away. Suddenly realizing her vulnerability, she reconstructed what she could of her composure. "I can't cry. The other guys'll think I'm a wimp."

I smiled as gently as I knew how. "Listen," I said, "it doesn't matter what others think. Anyway, they all want to cry too. You're being a leader. Everyone in here is hurting. Some of them with bigger problems than yours or mine."

She looked at me with soft, moist eyes. "Do you really think God would help someone like me?"

Time after time I've found that the Ground Zeros of life either make you a bitter person or a better person. And the first step to becoming "better" is to ask that question that Maria asked. Then, believe the answer: "Yes, He will. All you have to do is call on Him."

As I mentioned, bitterness is an unholy alliance of anger, a sense of betrayal, helplessness, and hopelessness. But in my counseling ministry I've found that bitterness is spawned when you feel helpless and believe there's no hope for the future. A little later we'll talk about anger, and what to do about that sense of betrayal. Right now, though, let's tackle these other two. Let's discuss how you turn hopelessness into hopefulness, and helplessness into faith and reliance on God. When you do, bitterness dissolves.

HOPELESSNESS TO HOPEFULNESS

First, let's increase your hope for the future. God tells us in Romans 8:28, "And we know that all things work together for good to those who love God, to those who are the called according to His purpose." This is plain language. God is telling us that if we throw ourselves on His mercy, if we trust in Him and love Him, He works for good in every aspect of our lives. If you find yourself out of work, and you trust in God and love Him, your time of joblessness will work out for the good. If your spouse has taken you for everything, if you love and trust in God, that human betrayal will work out for good. It doesn't mean the road will be without bumps and hairpin turns; it doesn't mean the outcome will be all roses and sunshine; it doesn't mean you won't be required to make some changes along the way—in fact, you probably will. But when the dust settles, and a relative calm returns, *good* will have resulted.

Some are quick to point out that the "good" is from God's perspective, not necessarily from ours. But what does that matter? If you have a child and you love that child, can you work out a situation in your life and call it "good" if you are better off and your *child* isn't? Of course not. If things work out *good* for God, they'll work out good for you. There is no greater hope than that.

May I offer another reason for hope from Romans 8:31-32? "What then shall we say to these things? If God is for us, who can be against us? He who did not spare His own Son, but delivered Him up for us all, how shall He not with Him also freely give us all things?" Not only will good result from whatever devastation has now befallen you, but it will be a great good given by a God who will "freely give us all things." You may never look back and say your Ground Zero was worth experiencing—particularly if you've lost a loved one—but one day you'll look back on the road you've traveled and you will be able to say a loving God was at work.

There is much to hope for, even within your Ground Zero.

HELPLESSNESS TO FAITH

Maria was right. In a sense she was helpless. So much of her life was out of her control. She had to follow orders on the job. She had three daughters who needed food, clothing, a place to live, love, understanding, discipline—all of which she had to provide every day. What her wayward husband did was out of her control, and if he became irritating—well, she couldn't do much about it. If she wanted to think of herself as helpless, she had a lot of evidence to back up her contention.

But there's another way to look at it. Instead of seeing herself as helpless to change the world she lives in, she can have faith in the Lord and see Him at work within her world, ironing out the bumps. She can throw her burdens into His outstretched arms and free herself up emotionally, even physically, to enjoy and gain fulfillment from her circumstances. In Matthew 6:26, Jesus tells us, "Look at the birds of the air, for they neither sow nor reap nor gather into barns; yet your heavenly Father feeds them. Are you not of more value than they?" In verses 28-30 He changes the image from birds to flowers: "Consider the lilies of the field, how they grow: they neither toil nor spin; and yet I say to you that even Solomon in all his glory was not arrayed like one of these. If that is how God clothes the grass of the field, which is here today and tomorrow is thrown into the fire, will he not much more clothe you, O you of little faith?" Jesus' point in talking about birds and flowers is this: we are valuable to God. If He goes to such pains to care for birds and flowers, He will certainly care for us.

As we come to appreciate God's love for us, our whole perspective on ourselves and on life can be transformed. If instead of seeing ourselves as helpless, we can turn to God in faith and trust, He will carry our burden. That doesn't mean that Maria can quit work and play all day with her girls. It does mean, though, that the chronic worry about providing everything can be set aside, and when she gets home from work she can begin to enjoy her time with the kids. And when her ex-husband irritates her, relying on the Lord will make it easier to let the irritation roll off her back. She'll have God helping her then. What does she care about her ex's feeble attempts to buy her daughters' love? She'll be at work planting the greatest love of all—God's love—in their hearts.

But God has promised more than just to carry our burdens—He's promised to give us the desires of our heart. It might be very difficult to believe that the terrible days you're experiencing now will somehow morph into what you want most in life, but that's God's promise. There is some small print about this. It should be consistent with God's desires—which means it's not a self-centered want—but God's desire should be your desire anyway. Your world can be a far better place than you might now even think possible. For Maria, for instance, as God's love comes into her life and the lives of her children, maybe one day soon she'll be able to love her ex back into the family.

There's another reason to turn to the Lord in faith and trust. God tells us in Ephesians 1:11 ". . . being predestined according to the plan of him who works out everything in conformity with the purpose of his will." God is a purposeful God, and although you may not yet see divine purpose in what you're going through, know that it's there. Except for Jesus, King Solomon has been called the wisest man who ever lived. In Proverbs 3:5-6, he gives us some very good, very free advice: "Trust in the Lord with all your heart, And lean not on your own understanding; In all your ways acknowledge Him, And He shall direct your paths."

If you're feeling helpless and that helplessness feeds your bitterness, turn to the Lord in trust and faith. Doing so isn't easy. It takes a lot of prayer, a lot of humility, and there will be many missteps. But in the end you'll cherish your helplessness, for it's the Fount of All Wisdom who now guides your life.

A bitter life becomes a better life when you invite the Lord to take His rightful place as the spiritual head of your life.

YOU'VE BEEN PREPARED

Earlier in this chapter I described the feeling of being ill-prepared for what I was about to encounter at Ground Zero. I was telling you the truth. When I first arrived and began to work, I honestly believed nothing had equipped me to help the human devastation I found there. But that wasn't entirely true. As I look back on it, I can see that the Lord had prepared me, at least to the point where, with His help, I could make a difference in the lives I encountered.

If you're feeling ill-prepared to deal with your Ground Zero right now, I'd like to give you hope. The same is true for you. At this moment, you undoubtedly believe nothing could possibly have prepared you for what's happened to you. But you'll soon find that God—a God who loves you, who knows the emotional, physical, and spiritual trauma you're now experiencing—has prepared you. As you pray, as you face this tragedy, whatever it is, you'll find yourself drawing on reservoirs of knowledge, experience, and understanding you may not even know you have.

Be forewarned, your reservoirs probably won't be enough. But that's said to bring hope too. For God is there to make up the difference. Just as I counseled Maria, ask Him for what you lack, lean on Him and trust in Him. There's no way He'll let you down.

CHAPTER 3
FRUSTRATION OR
FORGIVENESS?

And be kind to one another, tenderhearted, forgiving one another, just as God in Christ also forgave you.

Ephesians 4:32

Sunday evening was warm in New York City. Had this been a few weeks earlier, New Yorkers would have been flocking to Broadway to see *The Producers* or to Times Square just to marvel at the lights, or enjoying one of the small ethnic restaurants that seem to be everywhere you turn. And if they happened to be at Yankee Stadium it would be to wildly cheer someone in to home plate, or question some umpire's eyesight. But, of course, it was *this* time in history, and at Yankee Stadium the Prayer Memorial had wrapped up about 3 hours earlier and we had finally arrived at the beating heart of Ground Zero.

Even though I'd been at work in the city for nearly a week, I'd purposely stayed away from the site of the World Trade Center towers' collapse. No matter how much we did at the morgue and Family Assistance Center, there always seemed to be more to do, more people to listen to and encourage. So we kept returning. As that first week wore away, everyone had reached an overwhelming state of exhaustion. Exhaustion was just the state of things. Three elements of the work tired us. First, the work itself—the long hours, the long days, with no breaks, no place to slip away to, no escape—which we actually didn't begrudge at all. In fact, the one day I did have about eight hours off, I went back to help. Long hours are okay when you're working hard for a righteous cause, but even though we wouldn't have wanted to take time off, our finite energies were about sapped. Second, the potential of further terrorist acts and the relentless uncertainty that that possibility visited on everyone. Everyone, in spite of the weariness, had to stay alert. If you rested, you might miss something that could mean your life or someone else's. Third, even though America had been previously attacked (Pearl

Harbor, Oklahoma City) we were all acutely aware that this attack was unique. Not only did the sheer magnitude of the physical and human devastation dwarf those others, but it was delivered by a ruthless, shadowy enemy, one who can only too rightly be called *evil*.

GRASPING THE INCOMPREHENSIBLE

I'm not exaggerating when I tell you that when I first saw Ground Zero it took my breath away. I'm sure you've seen pictures—magazines, newspapers, television—pictures of the tortured girders, the mounds of pulverized debris. And you've heard others tell you those pictures conveyed only a glimpse of what it was really like. Those people were very right.

On December 30, 2001, 110 days after the attack, the City of New York opened a public viewing platform at Fulton and Church Streets. Open from 8 A.M. to 9 P.M., it was the first of four that were planned, each able to accommodate up to 400 onlookers. If you have the opportunity to go, you'll see something beyond belief, something that may change your life's perspective. Just as with those pictures, the Ground Zero you'll see from that platform is not the same in scope or impact as the Ground Zero of September 11 and those few weeks thereafter. Workers have worked twenty-four hours a day and have done a monumental job of removing the debris and clearing the area. Of course, they'll never clear away what happened there.

While I was there, I thought many times how important it is for America to see what I saw. How good it would be for the nation to grasp the gravity of the 9/11 moment and to understand the serious nature of the message it is still pounding out.

Let my eyes be your eyes for just a moment. The magnitude of the destruction was all but impossible to grasp when I first saw it up close—even the people who worked there day-in and day-out will tell you that. It seems like miles of twisted, anguished rubble in all directions. Gray and grayer, everywhere are deep caverns with steel-layered canopies. Here and there steam and smoke drift up in white columns, at times bent and knotted by wind.

But rubble is just rubble. What gives it emotion, especially pain, are the men and women who worked through it in a desperate hunt for survivors. Everywhere I looked they were digging and searching, climbing over this mound and lowering themselves into that pit. Always keen-eyed, always searching for whatever remained of their fallen countrymen. Hundreds did this. At times they looked like ants on a very large, very tortured hill, insignificant when seen against such a massive backdrop, yet all of them heroes in their country's eyes. And as they searched, an obvious foul odor radiated up and followed the direction of the wind.

When they completed an area search, construction workers came in to remove debris. They directed and worked an army of heavy equipment. Backhoes and tractors crawled up and down the pile moving "earth" and metal so that huge cranes that surrounded the base of the mountain could carry the debris to long lines of dump trucks and flat beds that waited to carry the debris away.

The sheer size of the pile—more than five stories high, several acres in area—was, well, unbelievable, overwhelming. But I've used those words before. As I sit here writing this, I'm trying to come up with words to somehow describe what I first saw there. But adequate adjectives don't come. Huge steel beams, cut and laid onto trucks, each piece weighing tons, twisted like paper, melted like wax. And not just one. Forests of them, stacked like kindling—like a huge, grotesque game of pick-up-sticks. And to think that human beings did this to other humans is still difficult to grasp. Months later I would see television video of Osama Bin Laden and his associates gloating about their success on 9/11. Standing there that first time, I still did not think it possible that man could do this to his fellow man, let alone laugh about it, and consider this ravaging of the innocent a success.

When the four of us chaplains arrived we introduced ourselves to the Chief of FDNY and made ourselves available. "Good," he said, "You're just in time. Put on hard hats, find yourself a marker and write 'Chaplain' on them in big letters, and get to work. Everyone needs to know that help is here. My men are exhausted. We all may not believe in God or the same God, but we all need His help." That said, he immediately dispatched us to the "pile." And right away there was plenty to do. The remains of firefighters were being removed from the right and the left side of debris, so we split up—two of us went right and two went left.

PAIN IN PERSPECTIVE

The Chief was right, we all need God and His help in situations that bring devastation, and I set about bringing God's love to whomever I met.

And I met quite a few. Several stand out in my mind from that first night, but none more than the policeman who'd run into one of the auxiliary World Trade Center buildings to rescue people. Then he returned to get more people out and was caught when the building began to fall. Hit by falling debris, he ended up being buried. Fortunately, he was pulled from the rubble. Unfortunately, he'd suffered broken ribs, a burn-scarred face, a twisted neck, a sprained ankle, and a broken arm. Now, days later, he was back at the scene that had inflicted so much damage upon him. When I came upon him he looked dazed and deeply troubled. He obviously needed someone to talk to. But when I approached him, he resisted my help. When I presented my card, he said he didn't want it, and when I showed it to him and told him to call me anytime, he pulled a fistful of other cards from his pocket—cards from counselors, chaplains, psychologists. You name it, he'd resisted it over those past few days. When I told him to call me twenty-four hours a day, six days or six weeks or six years from then, he opened up to me. He knew I meant it and that I cared. After talking for thirty minutes with him, I introduced him to one of my associates and waded into a crowd of workers not far away in the hope of doing some good there. A few minutes later, though, I turned to see the policeman walking straight to the pile, cursing angrily. I quickly caught up to him and put my arm on his shoulder and asked what had happened, what was he doing. "You're not flipping out on me, are you? I thought we had made some headway in our talking."

He stopped, looked at me with tormented eyes for just a instant, then literally put his head on my chest and sobbed. A little later, when the tears were brushed away, he told me his story.

About a month earlier his wife had left him and moved in with a firefighter. When it happened, he wanted to hurt the guy, tear him apart. But today he came to honor him. "He was getting people out of the tower when it came down. They tell me they just now found his ID, which means he's in there someplace." He pointed five feet away from us. "I'm not going to sleep until they bring his body out."

Concerned that he might lose it when they did bring the firefighter out and do something he'd later regret, I asked him what he was planning to do.

Looking at me with those same tormented eyes, he said, "I am going to stand at attention and salute him. That's what I'm going to do. I'm going to pay him the respect a hero deserves."

I could hardly believe what I was hearing. How amazing to want to get even and harm someone one day, then have so radical a change of heart that you want to forgive and honor him the next. I asked him, "You mean you're willing to forgive this man even though he stole your wife?"

He nodded. "I forgive her and I forgive him." He looked toward the rubble and the people digging through it. "What happened to me is so small compared to this."

This disaster has brought focus and perspective to so many varied situations and so many issues that have plagued tens of thousands of people's hearts and minds, just as it brought focus and perspective to this man—forgiveness.

MOVING TOWARD FORGIVENESS

In the King James Version of the Bible the word *forgive* is used forty-eight times and *forgiveness* seven times. Jesus spoke about forgiveness more than any other person in Scripture. This isn't all that surprising, since forgiveness was His divine mission. He came to die on the cross so that the whole world could receive forgiveness from God, His Father.

When teaching His disciples to pray, He said to God, "And forgive us our debts, As we forgive our debtors" (Matt. 6:12). He wasn't speaking about money, either. When we sin against someone, when we wrong them in some way, we owe them a debt. We owe them whatever it takes to make things right. If through negligence we've broken their window, we owe them a new window. If we take something from them, we owe it back. At the very least, when we wrong someone we owe them a heartfelt apology. And when someone wrongs us, they owe us the same. So when Jesus tells us to forgive us our debts and forgive our debtors, what is He saying? What is forgiveness?

When we forgive, we work to transform the negative feelings we have toward a person to wholesome, positive feelings. But feelings are only part of it. Instead of wishing the person ill, and wishing God had different admonitions about revenge, we sincerely wish that good might occur to the person, the ultimate good being the person might come to know Jesus as his or her personal Lord and Savior. We also work to reestablish an appropriate level of fellowship with the person.

Forgiveness isn't easy. In fact, I've heard it said, "Forgiveness would be okay if it wasn't people we had to forgive." Especially people we may not be too fond of, those who need forgiving. We've all struggled with forgiveness. Peter certainly did. Demonstrating his teachable spirit, he once asked Jesus, "Lord, how often shall my brother sin against me, and I forgive him? Up to seven times?" Jesus said to him, "I do not say to you, up to seven times, but up to seventy times seven" (Matt. 18:21-22).

Jesus is teaching us that you probably can't forgive your neighbor enough, no matter what he's done to you. Even if the person has stolen your wife or your husband. Forgiving seven times, as Peter suggested, even seems like a lot sometimes. Especially when it's the same person who keeps needing our forgiveness. Usually we'd have written that person off a while ago and would still be keeping a good distance from them. But we're not to do that. Instead, Jesus tells us we have to forgive at least 490 times (70 x 7). Some translations give the number as 77, but even 490—the larger number—isn't that significant in the grand scheme of the mathematical world. When we look at the context in which the number is presented, however, we see Jesus is revealing a truth. The truth appears to be this: when you feel that you have forgiven someone enough there is always room for more.

And when we don't forgive, often we find ourselves regretting it.

Years ago I counseled a lady who was furious with her husband. He'd had an affair and she was positive she could never forgive him. She counseled with me off and on for two years, and even though her husband had repented and was doing his best to become the man she wanted, she made good on her refusal to forgive and gave up on the marriage. After she left him she began to date many men. After a short while, she fell away from the church and went her own way. Four years later my secretary told me that an old friend called and needed desperately to talk with me. It was this lady. Interested to see where her life had taken her, I called her back quickly.

Her four years of "freedom" hadn't gone well for her. She'd become infected with HIV and had just learned it had turned to AIDS. I encouraged her and prayed with her and told her we wanted her to make our church her home again. Quietly the disease ate away at her until several months later I sat beside her bed in the hospital only hours from her death. Finally, on her deathbed she prayed and asked God's forgiveness for the sins of her life, and in the next breath she forgave her husband. How sad that the lack of forgiveness brought anger and the anger turned to bitterness, and bitterness brought death.

WHY FORGIVE?

When the Ground Zero of your life is the result of someone having wronged you, you must be willing to forgive. *Jesus said,* "For if you forgive men their trespasses, your heavenly Father will also forgive you. But if you do not forgive men their trespasses, your Father will not forgive your trespasses" (Matt. 6:14-15).

It is much like the law of sowing and reaping. If you sow forgiveness, you eventually will reap forgiveness. Although it may sound like a selfish reason to forgive, it's not. So often we get hurt and instead of sitting still, praying, and seeking counsel, we run off in all directions in an attempt to stem the pain and recover what we've lost. Instead we end up thrashing around without a purpose. In John Haggai's book *How to Win Over Worry,* he tells the story of a mother of eight in Darlington, Maryland. After returning from a neighbor's house, she walked into her living room to see five of her youngest children huddled in a circle, concentrating with great interest on something she couldn't see. When she finally discovered what they were looking at, she couldn't believe her eyes. Right in the middle of the circle were several baby skunks. She screamed at the top of her voice, "Children, run!" Each kid grabbed a skunk and ran!

We don't want to run from our Ground Zeros carrying things with us we should leave behind. Leave your desire for revenge, your bitterness, your negative feelings at the rubble—and take with you only the good. Don't continue a life of frustration when you can find healing in a life overflowing with forgiveness.

CHAPTER 4
THE HIGHER ROAD

Greater love has no one than this, than to lay down one's life for his friends.

John 15:13

At 8:45 A.M. (EDT) American Airlines Flight 11 out of Boston, Massachusetts, crashed into the north tower of the World Trade Center. About eighteen minutes later, United Airlines flight 175, also from Boston, struck the south tower. Like millions of us, you no doubt vividly remember the video footage—shown time and time again during that morning and the days that followed—of the planes ramming into the buildings, the flames exploding from gaping holes, the internal inferno spreading quickly inside as flames rode the streams of jet fuel down the steel spines, then the collapse of the towers.

I was told that as the second plane approached the south tower, an alert, self-sacrificing member of a government agency performed an incredibly heroic deed. As the plane, now a deadly missile, neared his office window, this agent set aside his own interest in self-preservation and placed a call to his agency's communications center. Standing there in harm's way, he described that plane in detail—type, color, identifying markings—just in case there were no videos of the incident and the plane disintegrated upon impact. At 9:03 a.m. this agent—along with so many others—was killed as this airliner carrying fifty-six passengers and nine crew members cut its horrific swath.

A HIGHER ROAD

When it appears the world is falling apart, most people's natural, knee-jerk reaction is to panic, think of self-preservation, and run—fast and far. They act without thinking, or they think of themselves before they think of others. This is normal and understandable behavior for all of us. After all, who wants to stay in a place where you're constantly being pounded by pain and anguish? Yet this hero of 9/11 reminds us there is often a higher road to take in life. Especially when those times are critical, and when other people's futures, perhaps even their very lives, may depend on our standing firm and confident. There is a prominent truth in the Bible that never wears out, rusts, or becomes impossible to perform, and it's proven itself over and over again for 2,000 years in the lives of millions of believers. It was written by the apostle Paul, a man who possessed remarkable credentials, good intellect, and proven character. We already talked about this truth in chapter 2, but it bears repeating. In Romans 8:28 we read, "And we know that all things work together for good to those who love God, to those who are the called according to His purpose."

What may be hard for us to grasp is that God sometimes uses our self-sacrifice as a means of making all things work together for good. Jesus said, "For whoever desires to save his life will lose it, and whoever loses his life for My sake will find it" (Matt. 16:25). And in Romans 5:7-8 the apostle Paul presented Jesus Christ as the supreme example of self-sacrifice: "For scarcely for a righteous man will one die; yet perhaps for a good man someone would even dare to die. But God demonstrates His own love toward us, in that while we were still sinners, Christ died for us."

Note that the people Jesus died for did nothing to earn His love. (In fact, they were sinners!) Yet He chose to give His life that they might live. This agent in the south tower represents what countless others—military and civilian—have done over the years in times of national emergency: stood firm, remained faithful to their task, did their duty, and gave their lives for others.

History has shown us repeatedly that in times of disaster and critical stress, people often rise to the top of a situation. These people generally don't see themselves as heroes, and when identified as such, they don't necessarily want a hero's accolades. When those accolades do come, their response is usually, "I did what any normal person would have done in the same circumstances." That's generally just humility at work. Too often, the "normal" person runs.

When faced with our own Ground Zero experience, we can feel trapped, carried along by events, with no options. But the truth is that, just like this agent in the south tower, we have options. We can choose the higher road, stand firm, and do what God has called us to do. Let's take a look at what that higher road is.

THREE ATTRIBUTES

I'd like to look at three attributes exemplified by this hero in the south tower, this professional servant. They are qualities that each of us, when faced with a Ground Zero in our lives, are capable of exercising. But the real question that faces us is whether we are willing to exercise these qualities. I have a friend who owns his own health club and is a certified weight trainer. He says the human body is a phenomenal machine. Our muscles, he points out, have memory. When we work out and develop our muscles regularly, they remember how far we've stretched them. If we fall away from our regular routine for several days, even for several months, when we resume regular workouts our bodies will respond as before. In the same way, as we exercise our character, that is, do our duty—the job God has given us—as often as we can, we'll find that when the chips are down, we're more able to reach down into the very depths of our inner being and scoop up all the character we'll need.

This Ground Zero hero shows us three attributes we should exemplify when facing adversity, even when it has got us right in its crosshairs. May this life that was lost on 9/11/01 live on in our minds as we learn from his steadfastness and professional demeanor.

PEACE OF MIND

This public servant had *peace of mind,* and that peace of mind gave him the presence of mind he needed to calmly describe the approaching airplane. The word "peace" is found in every book of the New Testament except one. It actually means a cessation of hostilities. It deals with harmony between people and tranquility in one's own soul and mind. It is obvious to me that this individual had peace of mind. There was no doubt that his professional training "kicked in" and he did what he was trained to do—he did his duty and became a good witness. Interestingly enough, law enforcement personnel often would rather a citizen keep out of a situation and just be a good set of "eyes" for the arresting or interviewing officer. Our hero in the south tower did just that.

It may seem incongruous to you to be at peace in a time of unbearable trouble, but God tells us peace is available for each of us when we need it. The Bible mentions the word *peace* 400 times. It is a major subject of both Old Testament and New Testament writers. In his closing remarks to the church in Thessalonica, Paul said: "Now the Lord of peace Himself give you peace always in every way. The Lord be with you all" (2 Thess. 3:16). In another text Paul calls our Lord "the God of peace" (1 Thess. 5:23). God is our ultimate source of peace—a peace which transcends all understanding, a peace He freely gives us.

Jesus said, "Peace I leave with you, My peace I give to you; not as the world gives do I give to you. Let not your heart be troubled, neither let it be afraid" (John 14:27). If anyone had the opportunity and a reason to be overcome by fear—the prospect of being crucified while carrying the sins of the world, the prospect of having His Father forsake Him—and give in to that fear, Jesus did. Yet, instead of being overwhelmed by fear, He became the reservoir of all courage and peace, the sweet river of peace from which we may come and freely drink when we are in need.

I clearly remember the day when I was thirteen years old and my mother came home early from work and asked me to join her for a drive. My mother and stepfather owned a nice boat and kept it moored in a boathouse on the Columbia River, the border between Oregon and Washington, not far from the Portland International Airport, and we were headed in that direction. "I have some bad news for you," she said. I asked what it was. "We are going to remove some of our personal belongings from the boat. Your stepfather is leaving and we are getting a divorce."

Whether you are an adult, adolescent, or child going through the torment and pain of a home breaking apart, as I was at thirteen, or if some other crisis has come pounding at your door, you need a foundation of peace upon which to rest. From this peace we gain the courage and presence of mind to face the onslaught and complete our duties, the jobs God has given us to do.

So often, when our world collapses around us, anger, bitterness, and discouragement can crush the human spirit, sometimes taking us mere mortals beyond the point of no return. We lose our resilience and give up hope. But when we have God's peace ruling in our hearts and lives, we too can pick up our cell phone and call headquarters and do our jobs right to the last.

SACRIFICE

The second quality, an obvious one, is *sacrifice*.

Standing there at the window, the nose of that plane aimed right at him, the agent knew what he was about to give up. Yet he stayed. Not one of us would have belittled him if he'd dashed for the stairs. But he was *sacrifi-*

cial—in heart, attitude, and action. Trained to gather and assimilate information and to use all his senses to bring a case to conclusion, to bring justice to an unjust world, making that phone call was all he could have possibly done—it was *first* nature to him, like breathing. He was a true professional. His concern was not for himself, but for the good of all.

In my case, I know that my mother sacrificed a lot as she raised two boys on her own. The teen years for my brother and me could have been much harsher and far more difficult had it not been for her. She, like this agent, sacrificed so much of herself to do the job God had given her to do. In her case, she made sure her children had the opportunity for solid, adult lives usually reserved for the children of intact families.

SELFLESSNESS

Our south-tower hero displayed the ultimate act of *selflessness*.

When trouble storms in, it's common for those affected to become self-centered, to erase their concern for others and focus on themselves and how the storm is affecting only them. For instance, if they're suddenly fired, their first reaction is to discount how their own poor work habits contributed to their job loss, and instead blame their boss. He's a jerk, out to get them. Or when bad news comes, instead of looking around to see who else they can help through the tragedy, they curl up, knees to their chin, and cry. When major tragedy knocks the wind from their sails, it seems normal to turn inward, put up their defenses, keep their pajamas on, and just stay in bed—perhaps for the rest of their lives.

We can't let true pain and emotional suffering turn into self-pity. Here's what God says about it.

King Solomon referred to these times in our lives when he wrote in Ecclesiastes: "To everything there is a season . . . A time to weep, and a time to laugh; a time to mourn, and a time to dance" (Eccl. 3:1, 4). Weeping and mourning are natural reactions when our world falls apart. We should never feel embarrassed or guilty that we weep and mourn. It's important for us to openly express our feelings. In fact, experiencing the profound sadness weeping reveals is necessary to a healthy mourning process. And mourning is from God. It comes so that we might heal after the tragic loss of anything and anyone we've held dear. "Weeping may endure for a night, But joy comes in the morning" (Ps. 30:5).

God wonderfully created each one of us and made each element of our bodies—including tear ducts—for a purpose. The tear ducts are two small openings at the edge of our upper and lower eyelids. About six percent of children are born before their tear ducts open. Ninety-five percent of those tear ducts open on their own before the child's first birthday. Which is good, because before they know it, life *will* happen, and tears *will* come. Produced by numerous glands that populate the insides of the eyelids, our tears drain away from the eye through these ducts. Milked into these openings when the eyelids blink, they drain through narrow tubes to a sac under the skin at the inside corner of the eye. Tears then drain into the nasal cavity. This canal system is phenomenal in design and shows that God knew tears would be an emotionally healing function in our lives. Tears are designed to help us release pain and emotion; it's therapeutic for us to cry.

But crying can possibly take over our life. Healthy mourning can give way to self-pity. And when self-pity gains control we focus only on ourselves and how the situation affects only us—but even that limited perspective is distorted, generally warped and clouded by fear and apprehension. Our perspective clears and broadens, though, when we turn our emotional eyes outward. The moment we do, we begin to see the crisis in its fullness and become aware of others who've been affected. Instead of the crisis overwhelming us, as we might expect, the command God gave us to love begins to work in our hearts. Instead of reeling back, we reach out to those around us in selfless acts of caring. Instead of lashing out at people or withdrawing behind protective walls, we begin to manage the problems we face with a sharp sense of purpose. That had to be what happened with our hero agent.

This has to be what my mother decided to do years ago. She realized her sons were more important to her than revenge, anger, or bitterness. In her eyes we were also worth an extraordinary amount of time, and she did her best to dedicate herself to her boys. Not only was she there for us whenever we needed her, but she never missed a football game, wrestling match, or track meet that my brother Kent and I played in—even the day games, when she had to make up those many hours at work. What a sacrifice! What a selfless attitude!

One of the most widely known illustrations Jesus gives concerning selflessness is the story of the Good Samaritan. Let's take a look at it.

A certain man went down from Jerusalem to Jericho, and fell among
thieves, who stripped him of his clothing, wounded him, and departed,

leaving him half dead. Now by chance a certain priest came down that road. And when he saw him, he passed by on the other side. Likewise a Levite, when he arrived at the place, came and looked, and passed by on the other side. But a certain Samaritan, as he journeyed, came where he was. And when he saw him, he had compassion on him, and went to him and bandaged his wounds, pouring on oil and wine; and he set him on his own animal, brought him to an inn, and took care of him. On the next day, when he departed, he took out two denarii, gave them to the innkeeper, and said to him, "Take care of him; and whatever more you spend, when I come again, I will repay you." (Luke 10:30-35)

Selflessness simply means to set aside your own interests in favor of the interests of someone else. Sometimes it can be someone hurting. Samaritans and Jews were enemies. A lot of hatred existed between the two groups. Yet this particular Samaritan was willing to help the injured Jew anyway, even though it would be at his own expense. This selfless man sacrificed time, money, and tradition to bring healing in a painful situation.

WHAT ABOUT YOU?

Do you want to run in the face of your Ground Zero? Do you want to find somewhere to hide until your world gets back to normal and the pain subsides? Maybe you want to be like the firefighter who lost himself in alcohol in order to deal with being abused as a child, or like the policewoman who built walls of bitterness to protect herself from dealing with the pain of her husband deserting her and their three daughters.

Sometimes it's appropriate to run in the face of disaster—in the event of a fire, for instance. But even in the face of an immediate danger like that, it's important to keep your wits about you and have the presence of mind—the peace of mind—to make that telephone call. Are there others around you who need your help—children to protect and nurture, friends who count on you, an employer who trusts you to do the right thing? That doesn't mean you're foolhardy and take unnecessary chances, but do you need to set aside your own interests for a while to meet the needs of others? Can you be the example of God's love to someone also touched by the tragedy? Yes? It's time to exhibit peace of mind, sacrifice, and selflessness. And if you can do so, in your actions you will find the peace that brings healing and hope.

Psalm 46:10 says: "Be still, and know that I am God."

Life's road is often filled with unexpected twists and turns, surprising situations that test our resolve. To complete this journey we're on, we need the patience to allow the situations in life to unfold naturally. The further off September 11, 2001 becomes, the more we're able to cope with the dastardly deeds committed that day. My pastor, Chuck Smith, always has said, "Time is a great healer." The same will be true for your Ground Zero. As time moves on you'll begin to regain a sense of normalcy.

It was exactly sixty days after I had returned from New York City when I realized I was beginning to think "normal" thoughts again, those I remembered thinking before I went to New York. It takes time for wounds to heal.

What wounds?

Stress, emotional strain, traumatic situations, disaster, critical incidents, and personal problems—all are like physical wounds. They cut deeply into our souls; before we feel right again, they need to heal. And when time has closed the wound, though we may remember our Ground Zero, our lives will go on.

How can we find peace?

1. Begin by praying to God and asking Him for peace.
2. Start reading the Bible and finding peace in the comfort of Scripture.
3. Be open and honest with yourself and your feelings.

Notice in the following Bible verse the word "multiplied." Peter didn't want to add, subtract, or divide peace from his readers. He wanted to make sure that peace was multiplied to them. And this multiplication would come to them through the knowledge of God and Jesus our Lord. "Grace and peace be multiplied to you in the knowledge of God and of Jesus our Lord" (2 Peter 1:2).

How can we live a life of sacrifice?

1. Look beyond yourself in the situation and think of others
2. Read the Gospels and learn of Jesus' sacrificial life
3. Let love control your thoughts and actions.

The Apostle Paul saw Jesus as the ultimate sacrifice for us, making Jesus our role model for sacrificial living. He wrote this word of encouragement and exhortation to the church in Ephesus. In it he speaks of godly living using Jesus as an example. "And walk in love, as Christ also has loved us and given Himself for us, an offering and a sacrifice to God for a sweet-smelling aroma" (Eph. 5:2).

HOW CAN WE LIVE A SELFLESS LIFE?

1. Take the following Bible verses to heart and put them into practice when you recognize your world is falling apart.

"Let each of you look out not only for his own interests, but also for the interests of others" (Phil. 2:4).

"Then Jesus said to His disciples, "If anyone desires to come after Me, let him deny himself, and take up his cross, and follow Me" (Matt. 16:24).

2. Finally, when the Ground Zeros of life come our way, we must be willing to be givers, not takers.

We thank God for people like the selfless agent on his telephone. May we learn to take the higher road in life. Jesus said, "Greater love has no one than this, than to lay down one's life for his friends" (John 15:13).

CHAPTER 5
COMMUNICATION

A word fitly spoken is like apples of gold in settings of silver.

Proverbs 25:11

The whole world waited expectantly for the advent of Y2K—the year 2000. At precisely 12:00 A.M. (midnight) on January 1, 2000—bang!—computers around the world were to crash, possibly launching nuclear missiles and bringing modern civilization to an end. Obviously, it was an empty concern. The date came and went with very few computer "hiccups." Waiting on the horizon of the new millennium, though, was an event we didn't foresee—the September 11, 2001 attack on the United States by suicide pilots flying hijacked airliners.

With close to 3,000 confirmed deaths from this atrocious act of terrorism—in the planes, the Pentagon, and the World Trade Center, including innocent civilians and the Muslim extremists—this day of infamy ranks as the greatest loss of American lives in history inflicted by a foreign enemy. The attack on Pearl Harbor on December 7, 1941, claimed 2,388 American lives. On June 6, 1944—what has come to be known as D-Day—a total of 1,465 American soldiers died.

The only bloodier day came in another September, on the 17th, in 1862, when we inflicted 4,700 casualties upon ourselves. That was the Battle of Antietam, during the Civil War.

COMMUNICATION IS CRITICAL

Just as communications were important at these three battles, communications were even more important on 9/11. Why? Because over the years we've come to rely so heavily on communication technology. We've come to expect our phones to work, our televisions fed by satellite and cable to work, our cell phones to work—and work in all environments, from somewhere below the city streets to the tallest high-rise, even from planes flying at 30,000 feet, and in all situations, from picnics in Central Park to emergencies.

When the World Trade Center and the Pentagon were attacked on 9/11, Americans experienced one of the most severe emergencies in their history.

And just as the attack snuffed out many lives, it also took with it lower Manhattan's desperately needed communications.

And no wonder. Atop the north tower sat a host of microwave and satellite substations, each carrying millions of calls. Not far from the towers, and caught in the path of destruction when the towers collapsed, were the Verizon telephone offices and equipment center. When their equipment was damaged, phone service deteriorated even further.

Lower Manhattan, from south of 34th street, went communication silent. Had this been a quiet Sunday afternoon, and this loss of service had resulted from a decayed trunk line, it would have been extremely inconvenient. But with thousands and thousands of people trapped in a spreading inferno, and millions of others trying to deal with the worst attack on U.S. soil in history, this loss of service quickly became catastrophic.

New York Police Department Headquarters lost all telephone communications. This crippled the NYPD when they were needed most. Police quickly turned to cell phones, but that service soon got overwhelmed and became unstable. Good and clear communication is vital during a crisis.

Communication is also important to record the tragic and poignant history of the event. My heart was wrenched, as I am sure yours was, when I listened to radio and television news shows play the tapes of emergency dispatchers talking with people frantically calling for help from the World Trade Center. One woman who knew that the smoke was choking her and the others on her floor began to describe to the operator what was taking place in her office. Then she calmly said, between her chokes and coughs, "People are jumping out of the windows." Calmly, professionally, the dispatcher responded—very brokenly and very humanly—"People are jumping out of the windows?"

Days later, mobile cell-phone antennas were set up throughout the city. But even so, it was impossible for weeks afterwards to communicate clearly via cell phone. Either we couldn't get the number at all, or voices would suddenly just disappear. A two-minute phone call would take thirty minutes or more as we dialed and redialed and redialed again.

Just as communication was vital on 9/11 and those critical days that followed, it's also vital during those Ground Zeros in our own lives. Even when communication is stressful, even ugly, it is profoundly important *that* we communicate during these critical times—and *how* and *what* we communicate can make the difference between making it through a situation and falling apart.

My years as a pilot help to illustrate this. From the beginning, I was taught to navigate first and communicate second. In short, just fly the airplane. In an emergency, get the plane stabilized first. Don't just grab the microphone when trouble strikes and start screaming into it. First, stabilize the plane, fly straight and level, and avoid any terrain or obstacles. Then, only after things look better, you talk to the controller and tell him if you want to declare an emergency or not. For over 35 years of flying I've heard pilots say, "Don't ever declare an emergency unless it is really necessary."

"Why?" you ask.

"Well, because you'll have to fill out all kinds of paperwork and have the FAA asking you a bunch of questions."

I can't imagine a dumber response. I would rather declare an emergency and have all the assistance I can muster to help me survive the potential collapse of my world. Then, when I'm safely on the ground, filling out all those papers, I want to give that FAA inspector a big hug and thank him for a system that saves lives by helping people like me in difficult times. To those pilots, questions and paperwork are killers—when in reality they could end up killing themselves by not asking for emergency assistance.

A lack of communication often puts people at odds who don't have to be. Consider people facing financial collapse. Rather than talking to their creditors, they become embarrassed and hide when they find themselves unable to pay their bills. Then they continue to remain silent while their finances implode. I know several loan officers at our church. They tell me that if their customers find themselves in that situation and talk to them about it, in most cases their obligations can be restructured so the worst-case scenarios don't occur, and their financial lives can be revitalized. Unfortunately, people's pride will often hinder them from asking for help during a down time like this. And in the end, what options does a lender have? The lender has to turn the account over to collection. Soon interest and collection fees mount up, and the debtor may feel overwhelmed. They certainly feel guilty and hopeless. Bankruptcy can easily follow.

Not only is good communication important to our financial lives, but in every other aspect of our lives as well—family, marriage, education, work, and our relationships with others. It's also critical for globalization, politics, manufacturing, product and information distribution, and every other arena.

How Do We Communicate?

That said, how do we communicate? Usually we think of communication as two people talking face to face. But communication is far more than that. Jesus proved that by the way He chose to communicate. He often spoke to the crowds in parables. My good friend Chuck Butler led a band named Parable. The title of the group's first album was: *PARABLE (more than words)*. I have always liked that description of the term. Jesus, who spoke in parables, definitely spoke in *more than words*. You and I also communicate with more than words. We, too, tell stories, use analogies and visual images, but more than anything we speak with our actions. And since we were children we've heard that "actions speak louder than words."

I began to be affected by the lack of telephone service in New York City immediately after the Twin Towers collapsed. While at Ground Zero, the morgue, or the Family Assistance Center, while talking to those there with me, it dawned on me that people often find their worlds collapsing because of poor communication. And if it wasn't poor communication that actually caused the collapse, it certainly adds to the devastation that follows.

How different would our world be today if the Muslim extremists who piloted those planes, who carried out the murders of so many innocent people while killing themselves, could have sincerely communicated their feelings and demands in a manner other than violence? What if they could have sat down with their political, economic, and spiritual counterparts somewhere in the world and come to an agreement to bring peace and resolution to the conflict—which their actions have only made worse? What if those who still live and are still plotting and murdering the innocent could likewise communicate the yearning of their hearts to the One who listens when people call?

They would have used words instead of their own blood, and words can be far more powerful. King Solomon spoke often of using the correct words to communicate and how the words we choose ultimately show others who we really are. We can learn some important lessons from Solomon.

Why Use Words?

The first attribute Solomon assigns to words is *power.* Allow me to quote some verses he, through the power of the Holy Spirit, penned.

A wholesome tongue is a tree of life,
But perverseness in it breaks the spirit. (Prov. 15:4)

The mouth of a righteous man is a well of life:
But violence covers the mouth of the wicked. (Prov. 10:11)

Words have the power to encourage, inspire, direct, pull someone who's in danger back from the edge of a cliff, bring peace, and—their ultimate purpose—point people to Jesus. Life, true life, is brought by words.

Reckless words pierce like a sword,
but the tongue of the wise brings healing. (Prov. 12:18, NIV)

Words of apology, words that express deep longings for reconciliation, words of forgiveness, words that bring the hearer an awareness of God's rich tapestry of love, all bring healing. They apply cooling salve to inflamed emotional and spiritual wounds and bring warm reconnection while sustaining and revitalizing the ties—some threadbare and strained—that bind family and loved ones together.

Next, Solomon understood there is *value* in words.

There is gold and a multitude of rubies,
But the lips of knowledge are a precious jewel. (Prov. 20:15)

A word fitly spoken is like apples of gold
In settings of silver. (Prov. 25:11)

In both of these verses Solomon points out the value of what words bring. Gold and precious gems might prop up the estates of the rich, but you can have all the gold in the world and have a desperately poor soul. You can have all the oil in the world, yet still be searching for a sense of fulfillment, of meaning, of connectedness with the only Person in the universe who matters. You can have the ability to buy everything, the cattle on a thousand hills, and still not be able to buy the peace God gives. Without God and the salvation offered by His Son, gold and precious jewels are just things to be thrown away, things on loan to you while you breathe, things that may bring temporary comfort to the body and temporarily feed the ego—might even allow you temporarily to exercise a measure of power—but they will never end the permanent longing our hearts have for a sense of purpose. Only words pointing us to Christ can bring meaning in a universe so vast we can never hope to grasp it. Such words are valuable indeed.

When we take to heart the power and value of our words, we've taken that first step toward becoming a good communicator—we know how important words are. But the purpose of this book isn't to make you a competent toastmaster; rather, the skill I want you to hone is to better communicate when you're in pain.

When we *are* in pain, when our hearts are boiling with it, words seem so inadequate to describe the depth of our suffering. After all, they're only words, sounds and letters—not the anguish, not the confusion, not the knot of anger and fear growing in our stomachs. And sometimes they truly are inadequate. Who can possibly describe the emptiness we experience at the loss of a child or spouse? Or the depth of our sense of betrayal when we learn of a loved one's unfaithfulness? So if words so inadequately describe what we're feeling, why utter them?

Words also seem so useless at times like these. What good is it to reveal our pain? Will talking about it relieve it? Will anything be resolved? Will sharing it lighten our burden? And what of the burden we're placing on others? Now they not only have their own baggage to drag around, they have ours as well.

But in spite of these concerns, it's important that we do communicate our pain. The firefighter we met in chapter one illustrates this. He was overwhelmed by the sheer magnitude of destruction and the enormity of the rescue effort at Ground Zero. As he became increasingly exhausted, both physically and emotionally, the pain at the depth of his heart swelled until it was too massive to hold in any longer. He had to let it out. And when he did, he wisely compared the collapse of the World Trade Center to the collapse of his own life as a child. There was both power and value in his words, for while he reached out for help and comfort, I heard he was in tremendous pain. God sent me to help him.

COMMUNICATION IS SHARING

Jesus more effectively taught the world how to communicate than anyone before Him or since. Speaking one day to a group of men who didn't really want anything to do with God, he said, "For out of the abundance of the heart the mouth speaks" (Matt. 12:34). Over years of counseling I've taken these words to heart. They've taught me to listen carefully to the words spoken, for those words reveal the condition of the person's heart.

The original New Testament language uses several different words for communication. All have their root in giving and receiving or sharing. Generally we think good communication is talking, using all the right words and inflection, getting everyone in the room to understand the point—like giving a good speech. Not entirely. Good communication occurs during an exchange of ideas, a sharing of thoughts. I say something, you respond. It's a dialog. And it's within that sharing, that give and take, that meeting of the minds, that healing often takes place.

In the old days communication was reasonably simple—talking face to face, a fast pony, and the written word were about it (well, sometimes puffs of smoke on a tall hill). Now, however, communication has become a complex, highly technical skill. The United States even has a governmental organization dedicated to it, The Federal Communications Commission. We communicate via radio waves—AM, FM, and short wave. We have megahertz both low and high frequency. We use handheld devices and headset devices. We communicate through television, both UHF and VHF. Today we are on the verge of high definition television (HDTV). We have CDs and DVDs, VHS and Beta tapes, Digital 8 and High 8 tape. Add books, magazines, pamphlets, flyers, tracts, and newspapers. We communicate through computers, satellites, laser technology, music, drama, dance, and art. But even though communication methods and devices besiege us, beeping and yipping at us like impatient puppies, the issue still remains: How do we communicate on a personal level? And without a doubt, when our Ground Zero hits, we need to communicate and communicate quickly—face to face, fast pony, or smoke signal—and we need to communicate simply and truthfully, just as that firefighter did.

As in all life's issues, the Bible helps us here, too. So as we finish this chapter, let's take a look at a few of the communication tips it gives us. Then we'll take a look at the greatest communication tool ever given to mankind.

COMMUNICATION TIPS FROM THE BIBLE

First let's take a look at Peter, who gives us an example of quick, concise, direct communication. He's in a fishing boat with the other disciples on the Sea of Galilee and a powerful storm blows up. It's night and undoubtedly pitch dark; the only light comes from their feeble lanterns. Jesus has been praying on a nearby hilltop, and when the storm strikes He becomes concerned for His friends. Rising from His knees, He walks to the shoreline. But He doesn't stop there. Without missing a stride, He steps onto the water and strolls toward His frightened friends, the storm boiling all around Him. Seeing Him, Peter and the others suppose a ghost is about to pay them a visit. So they do what we'd all probably do: they panic. Peter, though, sees something that intrigues him, and he calls out, "If that's you, Lord, bid me to come." Responding, Jesus calls Peter out of the boat and Peter begins to walk on the water toward Jesus. What an experience that must have been! But Peter suddenly begins to see where he is. He becomes aware of the high and powerful waves churning around him, the wind screaming in his ears, and the stiff spray stinging his face. Fear sets in. Peter takes his eyes off Jesus and immediately begins to sink. He cries out, "Save me!" Hearing this cry for help, Jesus takes him by the hand and lifts him up, putting him back into the boat. (See Matthew 14:22-33.)

"Save me!" A short, pithy request. But it was clear and concise, and it brought Peter what he needed and the result he desired. Often when we're at our lowest point, when we have no idea how to articulate our needs—we just know they're huge—simply telling those near us "Help me" or "Save me" is enough of a first step to begin the process of getting the help we need.

Sometimes when life seems to gang up on us, when it's got us down on the turf and is piling on, it's almost impossible to communicate (in word or deed) anything positive. The Bible gives us an example of this in 1 Kings 17:8-16 when it tells about a poor woman. She was short on cash, with a young son to support. She was not in a very positive mood at all. God, seeing her plight, sent a messenger to her for encouragement and for a quick (albeit three-year) lesson in faith. Faith allows you to go beyond yourself and allows God to work when your world is collapsing. Although this woman needed food, she needed faith even more. Elijah was the messenger and God spoke though him.

> *Then the word of the Lord came to him, saying,*
> *"Arise, go to Zarephath, which belongs to Sidon, and dwell there.*
> *See, I have commanded a widow there to provide for you."*

So he arose and went to Zarephath. And when he came to the gate of the city, indeed a widow was there gathering sticks. And he called to her and said, "Please bring me a little water in a cup, that I may drink."

And as she was going to get it, he called to her and said, "Please bring me a morsel of bread in your hand."

Then she said, "As the Lord your God lives, I do not have bread, only a handful of flour in a bin, and a little oil in a jar; and see, I am gathering a couple of sticks that I may go in and prepare it for myself and my son, that we may eat it, and die."

And Elijah said to her, "Do not fear; go and do as you have said, but make me a small cake from it first, and bring it to me; and afterward make some for yourself and your son.

"For thus says the Lord God of Israel: 'The bin of flour shall not be used up, nor shall the jar of oil run dry, until the day the Lord sends rain on the earth.'"

So she went away and did according to the word of Elijah; and she and he and her household ate for many days.

The bin of flour was not used up, nor did the jar of oil run dry, according to the word of the Lord which He spoke by Elijah.

When your world begins to fall apart, as this woman's world did, remember: God has sent you a messenger, His name is Jesus. Call on Him; trust in Him. He'll help in your time of need and, as He helped this woman, He'll provide *what* you need. As you walk along this narrow, yet liberating, path of faith, you'll discover, again as this woman did, that God will release you from your trust in those *things* you've been trusting in—those *things* you can see, touch, and use—and begin to refocus your trust in *things of God,* the things you can't see, can't touch, and can never use up, things that are divinely reliable and divinely appropriate. This woman of Zarephath had put her faith in the flour and oil; when it was exhausted, so was her faith, so was her life. God released her from that reliance on other things, and she shifted her focus to God. The instant she did, God multiplied His blessing on her. For how long? Until the day she died.

THE GREATEST COMMUNICATION TOOL EVER

What is the greatest communication tool ever given mankind? It's a small, six-letter word. *Prayer.* That's right—prayer. Prayer is a clear and concise way to communicate our wants and needs. It's giving and receiving, sharing. When you pray, God listens; when God acts or speaks, you listen. And Jesus has promised that when you ask, you will receive.

Unfortunately, prayer has a strong "religious" connotation to it, which may make many people uncomfortable about praying. When prayer is considered a religious practice, it can seem irrelevant to people who don't care much about religion. And I can understand that. The media, television, and Hollywood portray prayer as something officiated over by priests in ornate robes swinging golden globes leaking ghostly wisps of odiferous smoke, or a minister in a cleric's collar speaking in *thee's* and *thou's* with arms outstretched, or a grandmother's old-fashioned superstitions.

Such images are misleading, distorted concepts about prayer. Prayer is a direct communication lifeline from our hearts to the heavenly Father. Our prayers are important to God and vital to us—they're not just a ritual we go through. Please understand this. When your world is falling apart, send your prayers with expedience. Remember Peter's watery ordeal? His panic made his prayer quick and concise, and Jesus responded. Prayer works the same for you. Peter didn't bow his head or clasp his hands or kneel or use some special language or tone of voice. He cried out from his heart. He needed help and he needed it immediately. And God responded. If you're in trouble, call out to the Lord from your heart. He'll hear and He will respond.

Let's take a look at prayer from God's point of view. Revelation 5 describes a scene in heaven. Jesus steps up to the throne of God to take a scroll from God's right hand.

The scene is moving, to say the least. Four angelic creatures and twenty-four elders bow before Jesus. Revelation 5:8 goes on to say, "Now when He had taken the scroll, the four living creatures and the twenty-four elders fell down before the Lamb, each having a harp, and golden bowls full of incense, which are the prayers of the saints." One hand held a harp, and the other held gold bowls filled with the prayers of God's people! And those prayers are said to be incense!

The Greek word for these bowls refers to a broad, shallow container or a deep saucer. And within them, the prayers are presented like incense—a beautiful fragrance before God, accompanied by the deep, luscious, flowing tones of a harp. This is a stunningly beautiful image. And the form and content of the prayers don't matter. They can be short like Peter's, or long and involved like a mother praying for a wayward child. They're brought before the Lord as gifts of honor and worship from His people. But not only are they a feast for the nose and ear, they also excite the eye and our sense of worth. Remember King Solomon's words? "A word fitly spoken *is like* apples of gold in settings of silver" (Prov. 25:11). Silver and gold are valuable, and when polished they gleam with deep, vibrant richness, beautiful to behold. This is how your prayers arrive and are handled in heaven, with importance, by the elders who once lived here on earth, the angels who are super-beings created to serve the Lord, and, of course, by God Himself. If you have never been prone to pray, this is the time to begin. When your world crumbles, you need a power stronger than you to help you put it back together again. You need an inner strength to make it through the day, the next week, and the following month. Communicate simply, clearly, and concisely to God in prayer.

Paul used these same concepts of sweet incense and sacrifice in connection with the life and death of Jesus Christ. "And walk in love, as Christ also has loved us and given Himself for us, an offering and a sacrifice to God for a sweet-smelling aroma" (Eph. 5:2).

When you pray, pray in Jesus' name. "And whatever you ask in My name, that I will do, that the Father may be glorified in the Son. If you ask anything in My name, I will do it" (John 14:13-14).

Listen to the words of James, the son of Joseph and Mary, a half-brother of Jesus. If anyone knew about prayer, it would be James. He grew up with Jesus and observed Him throughout his life as Jesus sought God in prayer. In James 5:13-18, the Lord's half-brother puts it this way.

Is anyone among you suffering? Let him pray. Is anyone cheerful? Let him sing psalms.

Is anyone among you sick? Let him call for the elders of the church, and let them pray over him, anointing him with oil in the name of the Lord.

And the prayer of faith will save the sick, and the Lord will raise him up. And if he has committed sins, he will be forgiven.

65

Confess your trespasses to one another, and pray for one another, that you may be healed. The effective, fervent prayer of a righteous man avails much.

Elijah was a man with a nature like ours, and he prayed earnestly that it would not rain; and it did not rain on the land for three years and six months.

And he prayed again, and the heaven gave rain, and the earth produced its fruit.

The greatest gift of communication is prayer. Use it. God will hear, and God will answer your prayers. Of course, you need to be patient. But to experience peace in the midst of a disintegrating world you need God's love. Always remember, God wants to talk to you and help you through what might now seem like a confused tangle of rubble and a field of insurmountable obstacles.

My grandmother was a remarkable woman, and led a remarkable, though hard, life. She became a Christian as a teenager. Her mother died when she was twelve and left seven other children behind. Her father was a wealthy businessman and farmer, and wasn't around much. He was in the state legislature in North Dakota and had a very busy schedule—one that didn't leave much room for eight children or for Christianity. My grandmother married a minister against her father's will and was never to speak with him again. When her husband was twenty-six years old he died, leaving her with three children and no money. She moved to Eugene, Oregon, with her children. She had to raise the kids in pretty harsh conditions. She worked, of course, taught in a one-room schoolhouse. Her youngest son died at age eleven, one day after my mother's birthday. But even for all the adversity, she found tremendous comfort in her faith. She knew God had brought her through the valley of the shadow of death. As she aged and struggled with what probably seemed like an endless string of worlds collapsing, she discovered the power of prayer and the presence of God within them.

Several years ago I was in Palm Springs, California, for a speaking engagement. An elderly woman approached me. "Mike," she said, "did you have a grandmother named Ella Olson from Eugene, Oregon?" I said I did. "Well, I went to church with your grandmother and also attended the Wednesday morning prayer meeting she held in her home. I just wanted to tell you, your grandmother could pray the shingles right off the roof!" Well, while those rafters shuddered under the force of her prayers, she was praying for me—every day of my young life, and especially during my struggle as a teenager. When she died at eighty-six, I performed the funeral. It was my first funeral ever and as a young minister it was an honor to officiate at it. I'd been the prodigal son, and her prayers had been so very instrumental in my return.

Who knows, maybe with a little practice, you can pray the shingles off your roof, too!

SECTION II:
RESCUE

CHAPTER 6
RESPECT

In that day shall a man look to his Maker,
And his eyes shall have respect to the Holy One of Israel.

Isaiah 17:7

Immediately after the Twin Towers were hit, Mayor Giuliani ordered a Family Assistance Center be set up in the National Guard Armory at the corner of 26th and Lexington. The city also used the Javits Center at 34th and 11th Avenue. If the walls enclosing the great hall in that armory could express the emotion, grief, and agony they witnessed, I suppose mankind would reconsider the atrocities it has committed upon itself—and any future destructive acts.

The family and friends of those who had worked in the Twin Towers, but whose fate was unknown, came to this facility. With them came many others who were missing loved ones who might have been in the towers that day—along with untold numbers of tourists, visitors, vendors, delivery people, and many others just passing by. All those relatives and friends came hoping for even the slightest shred of information to help ease their minds.

The Family Assistance Center was located in the main auditorium of the armory. It is very large, with high ceilings and a balcony, and was filled with tables from one end to the other. After we passed through multiple layers of security, we entered the great hall and the surging sound of voices, a sound like the boiling rapids of a fast-moving river. On the right was a sea of chairs, an area for those waiting to be interviewed by police and to fill out missing person reports. Those waiting faced a podium and a makeshift stage set up for the mayor and other officials to make public announcements and give periodic updates on the grave situation at hand. To the right of this area stood a big-screen television permanently tuned to a news channel. Next to that, children played. If memory serves, this area was established by the United Nations. Parents, grandparents, and others could leave their children here and be assured they were well cared for while they were being interviewed and filling out the necessary forms. Working our way to the back of the armory, next came tables and chairs dedicated to the mental-health professionals and those who wanted to talk to them. Set up at the far right and in the back of the building, the American Red Cross had set up the Spiritual Care Center. Here ministers, rabbis, priests, chaplains, and other clergy were screened for participation in the enormous task of helping and encouraging those touched by Ground Zero.

The Spiritual Care Center was also used for debriefing the spiritual-care professionals before they went home. These debriefings were important. Critical-incident stress-management training tells us to be sure to give everyone involved in a critical situation an opportunity to talk things out, to express themselves so that undue stress doesn't build up to critical levels.

RESPECT UNDER PRESSURE

It was Saturday, September 15, 2001, nearing midnight. We had been in the Armory since 9 A.M., and now the final group of spiritual servants was to be processed out for the day. We all sat in a circle, about ten clergy who'd been there for the final four-hour shift. I listened as each spoke.

Somewhere in the middle of the mix, a pastor gave the account of his day, mentioning a wide variety of people he'd counseled or just listened to. One story was of a woman he'd encountered who'd been in the first tower before it collapsed. She'd come down several floors with a very large group and had made it out along with the others without injury or trauma. As he told the story, a single word caught my attention.

In recounting his conversation with this woman, the pastor said she'd used the word three different times when talking with him. What word? R-E-S-P-E-C-T. I was exhausted, nearly asleep on my feet, but to hear this word *respect* repeated three times by a survivor, by someone who'd been rescued from approaching death, hooked me like a Columbia River Salmon heading up stream.

Although I usually kept my eyes open for any emotional scars afflicting the spiritual-care team, this story about "respect" had my complete attention. What exactly did this word *respect* have to do with a towering inferno?

When the people in the first tower began filtering from their offices toward the emergency exits, the air was charged with excitement—but also peace. Until then, I pictured people escaping a burning building by scurrying down the emergency stairs in a chaotic mass—pushing, shoving, screaming—every person for himself. Not here. People worked their way down in a cordial, orderly fashion. Had they not, it would have been a disaster. There wasn't much room in there; the emergency stairs were only about three feet wide. But even for all this, disruptions in the stairwell did occur. One of the ladies working her way down the stairs was obviously overweight, her body about as wide as the staircase, so she was unable to move very quickly. "When firefighters came rushing up the stairs," the pastor told us, "they hit this logjam."

"Were the people mean to her?" I asked. "Cruel or hurtful?"

I was surprised when he answered, "No! That didn't happen. Just the opposite." The lady he'd encountered said, "We knew we were all going to die, so we decided we would respect one another." Men near the overweight woman helped her so the firefighters could continue up the stairs. "There was a peace and a calm all around us," the lady went on to say.

Wow! What good news! Because of respect, the people in that stairwell, and everywhere else that respect for one another existed that day, displayed human dignity and self-control in a time of unparalleled crisis.

This story brought me great peace. Just to see proof that people were still caring and loving—and the fact that they were still willing to be patient and help one another—gave me silent hope. This wasn't the only story we heard about the respect and dignity that reigned in those emergency stairwells. I'm sure there were areas where people panicked, where they pushed and screamed; but to know that human dignity showed itself with respect for others clearly reveals to us that the terrorists have already lost the war.

The following poem is cynical. It does show the heart of some people during crises, though. When your world is collapsing and your Ground Zero looms right before your eyes, the real you will bubble to the surface.

> *I wish I loved the Human Race*
> *I wish I loved its silly face*
> *I wish I liked the way it walks*
> *I wish I liked the way it talks*
> *And when I'm introduced to one*
> *I wish I thought What Jolly Fun!*
> Sir Walter Raleigh 1861-1922

This poem definitely does not reflect the heart of God. Jesus said: "For God so loved the world that He gave His only begotten Son, that whosoever believes in him should not perish but have everlasting life. For God sent not His Son into the world to condemn the world; but that the world through Him might be saved" (John 3:16-17).

How should you respond to your world falling apart? The natural response is to run, to put the disaster zone as far behind you as you can. Yet we know there are those brave souls who don't consider themselves in times of calamity, but instead consider those who need help. Survival begins here, and here is where triumph over the situation carves its foothold. So don't run from your Ground Zero. You have made it. You are alive. You have a full life ahead of you. Don't give up hope, for hope is your stability for the future.

EXAMPLES OF RESPECT

In all my years of public service and ministry, I don't think I've ever seen such respect and dignity in one place at one time as I did while in New York City. It started with the mayor. Here was a man who had done a decent job leading one of the world's largest cities. In the months prior to 9/11 he'd been beleaguered by political issues that pulled his job approval ratings down. His marriage was on the rocks, his personal life under harsh scrutiny. And to top things off, he found himself in the battle of all battles: Rudolph Giuliani was diagnosed with cancer.

The Australian Broadcasting Corporation summarized this period in the life of New York City's mayor in one report: "Rudy Giuliani probably thought it was the fortnight he'd never have. That was all the time it took for the world to learn about his prostate cancer, his affair with an 'age appropriate' woman—and the fact that his wife has accused him of having a long-term relationship with yet another woman. While he's far from a sympathetic character—and New York's tabloids are having a field day—this is one of the few times a handful of people are feeling sorry for the Mayor of New York."

Even though all of that and much more was going on, New Yorkers forgot all of it when September 11th reared its ugly head. The mayor took the city's reigns and worked relentlessly around the clock. I would see him at all hours of the night and day, throughout the city, with his staff and advisors, walking briskly to their next meeting. This man gained the respect of millions of people, not only in New York City, but also throughout the United States and the world. Why? Because he had *respect* for the survivors and the suffering families of the victims of this horrific day of infamy. His personal Ground Zero didn't slow him down at all. Though his world appeared to be falling apart, he committed himself completely to the job at hand and became an icon of respect and compassion.

Traveling around the city I saw respect in so many ways. It wasn't that I was on the lookout for it, but I couldn't help but see the way people treated each other. On the streets, horns didn't honk all day and night like you'd expect. On the subways and in elevators, people were kind and cordial. In the restaurants, waiters and waitresses were personable, and if they knew you worked at Ground Zero, they wanted to "comp" your meal. Some have said this behavior was something very new for this city of millions, but whether is was or wasn't, the Big Apple had definitely become the City of Love and Respect.

Jesus said to him, "'You shall love the Lord your God with all your heart, with all your soul, and with all your mind.' This is the first and great commandment. And the second is like it: 'You shall love your neighbor as yourself.' On these two commandments hang all the Law and the Prophets" (Matt. 22:37-40).

Detective Carlos Aviles is the president of Police Officers for Christ in New York City. A veteran of 20 years, Detective Aviles took me around the city and introduced me to people I needed to know. One evening we went to the Ground Zero command center, only a few hundred feet from the epicenter of mass destruction, and met with police officers and firefighters who were taking a needed break. In that small gathering was a man I would see on television, newspapers, and magazines many times in days to come. His name is Lee Ielpi, a retired fireman with the FDNY. Mr. Ielpi has two sons, Jonathan and Brendan, both also FDNY firefighters. Tragically, Jonathan died at Ground Zero when the buildings collapsed. Mr. Ielpi came to Ground Zero every day. Since 9/11 apparently he hadn't missed a day. And it was not just for Jonathan that he came. He felt that 343 firefighters went into those buildings, and he was going to keep coming until 343 firefighters came out. This was one of the most poignant images of respect we witnessed.

Detective Aviles, working with the city and others, opened a rest facility just 100 yards from Ground Zero. It was a place where workers could come to just lean back and sit and rest. They could use the restroom, check computer e-mail, make phone calls, even take a nap. While they rested, they'd be served free hot meals. Located at St. Joseph's Church and later moved to St. Peter's, this spot was manned by volunteers from just about everywhere. From December 26, 2001 until March of 2002 our church in San Diego sent an eleven-person team every week to serve these weary rescue and recovery workers. Mr. Ielpi would take a breather here too. And often he didn't come alone. This amazing gentleman would bring the widows of firefighters with him. Then, as they all sat with hot cups of coffee, he'd comfort and console them. His gentle words, blending with the respect shown to them by the volunteers and members of Police Officers for Christ who would serve them, helped them find the needed peace in their hearts.

THE DIMENSIONS OF RESPECT

When you consider respect, consider these three dimensions of it and it will help see you through your own Ground Zero. The first dimension is *respect for yourself.* The second dimension is *respect for those around you.* The third dimension concerns *respect for those who've hurt you* or been the reason your world fell apart.

> *Though the Lord is on high,*
> *Yet He regards the lowly;*
> *But the proud He knows from afar.*
> *Though I walk in the midst of trouble,*
> *You will revive me;*
> *You will stretch out Your hand*
> *Against the wrath of my enemies*
> *And Your right hand will save me.*
> *The Lord will perfect that which concerns me;*
> *Your mercy, O Lord, endures forever;*
> *Do not forsake the works of Your hands.*
> (Psalm 138:6-8)

RESPECT YOURSELF

When our world falls apart, we often feel devastated, overwhelmed, shocked, and helpless—then anger, bitterness, confusion, and a sense of failure set in. These emotions are natural, yet in this fast-paced society we are taught that revealing our emotions is a sign of weakness. So we learn when tragedy comes to "stuff it." Of course, society's wrong, and unbottling our emotions is the way to make it through a painful situation. Consider this:

what if rescue workers didn't keep searching? What if their fears and doubts paralyzed them and their inaction caused all potential survivors to die trapped in the rubble? Something occurs in their hearts and minds that tells them, "Let's go for it!" They become selfless in their service, and all weak stomachs are gone for the moment. Why? Because they have *respect* for their fellow man, and deep inside they have a *respect* for themselves. This is what they draw upon; this is what enables them to continue on in such shocking circumstances.

You may feel you could have done something differently. You may think, "If I had just not said the things I said or acted the way I did, the other person would have not suffered." Or when your spouse confesses to you that he or she has committed adultery, your anger overwhelms your senses and you blow up. When the dust settles, no matter what your Ground Zero, respect yourself. Your Ground Zero didn't come because you're a loser. Nor did it come because you could never do anything right.

You see, Ground Zeros don't make heroes. When buildings and worlds collapse, courageous people aren't just created on the spot. Ground Zeros reveal what is already in a person's heart. They reveal to the world what we are already made of. One of the best-selling books of the 1970's was *The Right Stuff*. It told the story of NASA's astronauts, who had the "right stuff" to be spacemen. Just as the challenges of space flight revealed who had the right stuff, so our personal Ground Zeros reveal who we really are.

If you focus only on the bad side of your life, seeing only your failures and weaknesses, you'll never rise from the rubble and move to safety. Instead, realize the God your Creator has given you a life to live, and you need to live it to the fullest and enjoy it. When devastation comes, don't quit, for heaven's sake! Call out to God and He will rescue you; He will help you through the calamity. As you rely on Him, you too will have "the right stuff."

King David found this to be true. He was an adulterer, a murderer, a failure before the eyes of his family, and disobedient to God. Yet God called him a man after his own heart. David, like any of us, made mistakes, had setbacks and failures. But he was strong in how he saw himself in the arms of a loving God. He respected his life. Listen to his words:

> *How precious also are your thoughts to me, O God!*
> *How great is the sum of them!*
> *If I should count them, they would be more in number than the sand;*

When I awake, I am still with You.
(Psalm 139:17-18)

RESPECT THOSE AROUND YOU

When my oldest brother, David, died in an automobile accident, I couldn't imagine that the intense agony the loss brought me could ever be used for good. It was a black hole, and I entered it on August 19, 1959. My mother and surviving brother, Kent, were also filled with grief. That terrible accident knocked all of us down for the count.

A few days later, on a sunny day in Portland, Oregon, Kent and I drove over to his girlfriend's house. By then the word had worked its way through the other kids in our high school. Four of them stood in his girlfriend's front yard. They were just hanging out as we drove up. I remember very clearly a cute, petite blonde named Peggy walking up to me. "I am sorry to hear about your brother's death," she said. It was obvious then, and still is, that the kids there that day and all the kids we met in the coming days of a new school year, were uncomfortable. Not with Kent and me. They were uncomfortable with death. Without a doubt death is the worst Ground Zero any of us can face.

However, I also remember when my mother and father separated. Life became different for me then. Even as a preadolescent, I knew the kids with fathers were different from me. I could see it clearly at Little League games and later in high school. Kids whose dads were at the practices and the games and were members of the booster clubs always saw more playing time in the games. In my junior year of high school, Kent experienced this firsthand and it angered me. He was a far-above-average athlete, but found himself playing second string to a kid with less ability whose father gave a lot of money to the school's football program.

Being fatherless had its drawbacks to me, as well. I sensed them treating me differently. Yet today I give glory to God for all those hurts, emotions, and scars. They have made me much more sensitive to the hurts, emotions, and scars of others.

I don't know your personal Ground Zero, but may I encourage you, be respectful of the people around you. Often people just don't know how to act around you or what to say.

It's just one of those awkward elements of life. Though you might not know it, these same people are watching you and may be transformed by the grace and poise you exhibit under great pressure. People aren't dumb; they know you're hurting and secretly hope their lives will never be tested like yours.

RESPECT THOSE WHO HAVE HURT YOU

This is probably the most difficult item on the list. How in the world can we respect the Muslim extremists who perpetrated such a horrific deed? How can you show respect to a cheating spouse or an incompetent employer? Let me explain.

Dr. Sherwood "Woody" Eliot Wirt is one of my most favorite people. Woody recently turned 91 years old (our birthdays are both in March). He's as spry and active as a man much younger. He founded *Decision* magazine for Dr. Billy Graham and was a member of the Billy Graham team for two decades. Having written thirty good-selling books and starting numerous Christian writers guilds, he has a lot of success under his belt. Some years ago Woody gave me a dictionary for a Christmas present—not just any dictionary, but one that's about four inches thick and weighs ten pounds. It is *The Random House Dictionary Of The English Language, Second Edition Unabridged.* I call this the weightlifter/bodybuilder edition.

In researching the word *respect* I found that it has sixteen different definitions in its noun usage. Not all of those apply to this situation. For example, I am not suggesting you respect those who hurt you in the sense of "the condition of being esteemed or honored." That's not what those hijackers or maybe even your cheating spouse or incompetent boss deserve from you. Esteem and honor should go to people of integrity and moral character, to heroes and people who sacrifice for the good of others.

I'm suggesting you take the higher ground in the situation in which you find yourself. Don't lower yourself to the debased level of your enemy. Rather, take the more excellent route and let God bring justice in His timing and in His way. I'm not saying this is easy, but it is necessary to move forward in your life. *Respect* in this dimension is definition 4 in the bodybuilder edition: "differences to a right, *respect* for a suspect's right to counsel." Let your life be a life of dignity and honor like the people coming down the stairwell in the World Trade Center.

Vengeance is Mine, and recompense;

Their foot shall slip in due time;
For the day of their calamity is at hand,
And the things to come hasten upon them.
(Deut. 32:35)

CHAPTER 7
PEACE

Peace I leave with you, My peace I give to you; not as the world gives do I give to you. Let not your heart be troubled, neither let it be afraid.

John 14:27

There is something firefighters and police officers have in common—when everyone else is running out of a building, they're running into it. Whether there's a gunman inside or a three-alarm blaze, in they go. It's probably not part of their job description—that part of it that reads, "You must be crazy to join"—but their commitment to the people they serve isn't craziness at all. It's something special. Something that's made them the people we have admired since we were children. On 9/11 they gave us even more to admire them for. Because of their heroism, 9/11 produced a serious vacuum at the management level, not only with fire and police, but in the private sector as well.

Canter Fitzgerald, an investment firm, lost 700 employees when their offices were destroyed. The FDNY lost 343 personnel, many of them top management; the New York Port Authority lost 37 employees; the New York Police Department lost 23. But the list is far longer than this. Many other government agencies and private businesses, both foreign and domestic, also lost large numbers of employees at Ground Zero. These losses severely devastate an organization and create a blistering psychic trauma that rifles completely through it, touching employees, stockholders, vendors, associates, and family members. If it were not for the professionally trained rescue workers who stormed the Twin Towers' stairwells,\ with over sixty pounds of equipment strapped to their backs, there would have been thousands more gone that day, and the governmental, business, and national psychic trauma would be even greater. Let's take a look at what we can learn from such dedication to job and duty.

EVERYDAY HEROES

These heroic public servants bring hope to our lives—often when we need hope most. If our house suddenly bursts into flames, we know a fire truck is going to roll up with highly trained people to save the day. If we suddenly find ourselves in some other danger, we can dial 911 and a courageous, armed police officer will respond to rescue us. Even if we just break a leg, emergency vehicles will be at our side in minutes to whisk us off to the hospital to see the doctors and nurses there. Of course we don't think about this a lot—we certainly don't talk much about it around the dinner table. But when we get into a real bind, as so many of our fellow countrymen did on 9/11, we expect someone will show up with Superman attributes—strong, courageous, trained, talented, able-bodied, sharp-minded—to be our rescue when we need them.

Someone else is available to us as well.

When our Ground Zero occurs, usually the last thing we want to be is a hero. We're happy if we can take charge of our own deteriorating situation, let alone concern ourselves with someone else's. And this is reasonable. We don't need to run into someone else's building when our own is crumbling around our ears. In fact, at these times we need to become less heroic and more dependent—on God. We need to trust Him during life's catastrophes. And just like the rescue teams, He's standing by to answer His 911 calls—our prayers for deliverance. And when He shows up, He brings more than a hook and ladder with Him. He brings infinite resources—the power that formed the universe—to put to work on our problems. The apostle Paul made this clear in a letter he wrote to the Philippians. "And my God shall supply all your need according to His riches in glory by Christ Jesus" (Phil 4:19). Now that's a promise—from God to you. Therefore, you need to accept this promise and let it be used to help and strengthen you.

Following September 11th, the anxiety in the air crackled like high-tension lines. Fearing chemical, nuclear, or biological attacks, contingency plans were in place to seal off Manhattan immediately if one occurred. In the case of a biological attack, a quarantined area was designated to prevent the infected from moving into other neighborhoods and infecting them, too. But Manhattan was only one of the concerns. What if the terrorists hit one or more of the other boroughs? To protect against that, officials placed pockets of police in strategic areas outside Manhattan. In that way, the NYPD would be ready with teams close to the action, no matter where the action was.

If your world is falling apart, remember that God also has plans and the capability to come to your rescue. God has your best interests at heart and He'll work on your behalf to help you recover. As the Scripture says, "God shall supply all your need" (Phil. 4:19).

When we're face to face with extreme stress, we can go into a form of shock, a place where we're so stunned we don't know what to do or where to turn. One day I spoke with a police officer at Ground Zero who was working with a neck brace on. "A woman rear-ended me," he told me. "She hit the back of my patrol car." She hit him so hard, in fact, his head was driven into the steering wheel. He got a whiplash. The instant he straightened up again, he got from the car to talk to the woman, but he suddenly felt dizzy and disoriented. Afraid he might be about to lose consciousness and fall, he made it quickly to the curb and sat, his head planted between his knees. The woman, now seeing she had a policeman to help her, got out of her car, stepped up to him, and asked the question that had probably caused her inattention to the patrolman's back bumper in the first place: "Officer, can you tell me how to get to La Guardia?"

I chuckled with disbelief. "She really did that?" He could only nod. She really did. She was stunned; he was stunned. For both of them, reality took on a new meaning.

WHEN NOTHING'S NORMAL

If we face a Ground Zero, reality may take on a new meaning for us, as well, at least for a while. Especially if we come to believe our lives will never again be the way they were. When our minds flood with sorrow, grief, denial, and disbelief, it's common to think that we're going crazy, losing our minds. In critical incident stress management we're taught something quite reassuring, words that help people who are going through devastating experiences minute-by-minute, hour-by-hour, and day-by-day: "The thoughts you are having are normal thoughts, that any normal person would have in an abnormal situation." This is good news for most of us facing the confusion of a tragic situation. Our thoughts are the same thoughts any normal person would have. It's the situation that's abnormal.

It's easy to understand. We're used to having the elements of our lives in order. I can count on certain things. When I get up in the wee small hours of the morning, I don't have to clear the fog from my head to find the shaver; I know exactly where it is. And when I step out the front door, I see my car there in the dawn's early gray. When I do, I know all is as it should be. That's true for everything in life—every aspect of it revolves around its own frames of reference, various comfort points that tell us life is moving along as it should. Enter a tragedy—a Ground Zero. Suddenly things change, maybe *everything* that matters. And the comfort points change as well. Without them to anchor us, we can easily become confused, even disoriented. For an instant we wonder where we are, how we got here. We have to work at unraveling what the world's become and get it back to what it should be. But facing an abnormal situation is only one part of the puzzle, responding to it is the other part.

We may not know how to respond, but even if we don't, odds are firefighters and police officers do. They have the training, and although they can't leap tall buildings in a single bound or go weak in the knees when they're around kryptonite, they, as ordinary people, have been given a divine gift to respond to abnormal situations and survive.

Jesus' disciples were in abnormal situations more than once. One of the most dramatic was being caught in the center of a powerful storm on the Sea of Galilee. Wind clawed at their boat while waves pounded it and washed over the bow, filling it with water. Most of these men were fishermen and had grown up in Capernaum and other seaside towns. So they knew the water—and the storms. There was a time not long ago when my wife and I learned about them too. During a recent tour of Israel, we crossed the Sea of Galilee. I asked two brothers who commanded our boat about the weather conditions. Referencing this story about Jesus, I asked what a storm like that could do. "Well," said one of the brothers, "we were coming from Capernaum to the far side of the sea with our father several years ago. The lake is fifteen miles long and six miles wide and the trip usually takes forty-five minutes. This time it became a four-hour ordeal. The storm came up suddenly. It's the warm air of the eastern desert that creates such storms. It comes boiling over the ridge and drops down and collides with the cooler air off the lake, which causes an explosion of climatic change." After hearing this, it was obvious to me that the storm the disciples were in was quite violent. So violent, in fact, that they panicked and lost composure. Jesus, exhausted from His ministry to the local people, slipped into the back of the boat, found a pillow of sorts, and in spite of the growing storm, went to sleep. But as the storm intensified, the disciples became frightened and woke Him. "Master, don't you care that we perish?"

You may have friends who've recently become frantic about something. A child is lost, or a big bill has come in unexpectedly and caught them short—some storm is brewing up for them. This is your cue to be more sensitive than usual to these people. They are seeing you as a safe port in their storm, just as the disciples saw Jesus. And just as it gave Jesus an opportunity to teach, it will give you a similar opportunity. If your friend still needs to know Jesus, your opportunity is to point your friend towards Him. If your friend knows the Lord, your opportunity is to bring encouragement and help strengthen your friend's faith.

JESUS GIVES PEACE

If you are the one experiencing a Ground Zero—as the disciples perceived they were—and "frantic" describes your reaction to it, come to the Lord as the disciples did. Invite the Lord, as the disciples did, to take charge. After all, it wasn't wrong that the disciples were frantic—natural reactions are natural. They knew the danger those storms presented. There was a difference with this storm, though: Jesus was with them this time. It would have been wrong for them *not* to seek Jesus' intervention. Notice that Jesus, when awakened in the midst of this storm, wasn't frantic. He was resting. Resting in the center of a raging storm of hurricane proportions. He sat in the place reserved for distinguished guests. William Barclay tells us, "In these boats . . . the place for any distinguished stranger is on the little seat placed at the stern, where a carpet and cushion are arranged. The helmsman stands a little farther forward on the deck, though near the stern, in order to have a better lookout ahead."

I saw a documentary about "storm chasers" on the Discovery Channel. It described the large C130 Hercules turboprop airplane that flies through a hurricane's outer turbulence, right into the storm's center. The sophisticated equipment on board collects and transmits all pertinent data needed by the weather watchers and scientists on the ground for tracking and analyzing the storm. In the middle of the hurricane is the "eye." Within the eye of the hurricane is perfect calm and serenity. For miles around the eye's refuge, fierce winds rage—some blowing over 100 miles per hour—yet at the storm's center is a safe harbor. Jesus was not just *in* the eye of the storm on the waters of Galilee; He *was* the eye of the storm.

When you find yourself in a small boat in a big storm, you have two choices. You can either stay in the front of the boat with frantic fear at the helm, or you can move to the back of the boat where serenity and rest are found. No, it was not wrong that they said, "Master, don't you care that we perish?" What was wrong was there was a contradiction in the way they called Him *Master*. If they had truly known that He was the ultimate Master, they would have trusted Him and followed His example. After all, He had said to them, "Let's go to the other side." He hadn't even suggested the possibility that they wouldn't make it. How wonderful that we can take our fears to Jesus—our concerns about death, injury, or anything else. We can voice our deepest feelings and questions, and He will help us. His response was not what mine would have been: "Hey, can't you see I need to sleep?" Instead, "Then He arose and rebuked the wind, and said to the sea, 'Peace, be still!' And the wind ceased, and there was a great calm" (Mark 4:39).

It's interesting to note that Jesus' command was actually to tell the storm to "be muzzled." Sounds like He was talking to a person, doesn't it? I think Jesus put it this way to remind us that we have an enemy—an enemy roaming to and fro seeking whom he may devour, an enemy of our souls. The devil was behind the Sea of Galilee storm. He was obviously trying to stop Jesus and His disciples from ministering to the people on the other side, and particularly to a man in dire need of God's love and forgiveness who awaited salvation there. Often we forget that the devil desires to inflict spiritual damage in our lives. In fact, your crumbling world could have the devil's fingerprints all over it. Nevertheless, Jesus offers peace in what may be a horrific situation.

Don't forget, there's an unfathomable reservoir of God's love ready to gush in, a cool, soothing river ready to quench the flames that threaten you, then to scoop you up and carry you to safety. This reservoir is Jesus. The prophet Isaiah called the Messiah the Prince of Peace. Jesus gladly dispenses God's peace to all who need it. In fact, at His birth in that lowly manger in Bethlehem, the angels of God, when telling the shepherds about Jesus, filled the sky with this message:

> *Glory to God in the highest,*
> *And on earth peace, good will toward men!*
> (Luke 2:14).

The angels announced a message of peace for the entire world to receive. This peace is available today in any situation, anytime we need it.

And it's an enduring peace, one that will last through any Ground Zero you might face. How do I know this? Jesus gave us this promise: "Peace I leave with you, My peace I give to you; not as the world gives do I give to you. Let not your heart be troubled, neither let it be afraid" (John 14:27).

Just as firefighters and police officers run into buildings as others run from them, God runs into our burning building, wraps us in His fireproof arms, and carries us to safety. And just as 911 gets the bell in the firehouse ringing and the hook-and-ladder on the road, our prayers ask God to step in and take over. The fire and police rescue workers don't send out bills for their services either. Imagine how the poor might react if they received a bill from the firefighters who saved their houses! As it would be for any house, it might be cheaper for them to let it burn. Or what if you dialed 911 to report an emergency, and the operator responded by saying, "Sure I'll send the police, but what will you do for me in return?" Property taxes usually support the cost of all these services. They're free to the caller.

Well, the bill for God's services has also been paid already. His services are free to the caller as well. Jesus paid full price about 2,000 years ago on a Jerusalem cross. On that cross His blood paid for your salvation and your liberation from sin, and in doing so, enabled God's love to rule in your heart during your time of sorrow. So, invite Him to help in your time of need. The call is free, and the results are guaranteed.

"These things I have spoken to you, that in Me you may have peace. In the world you will have tribulation; but be of good cheer; I have overcome the world" (John 16:33). Anne Graham Lotz continued this thought when she said, "Jesus is our fireman. He rushed into the flames of hell to snatch us out of the hands of the devil."

GOD'S RESCUE SQUAD

Remember, God has His emergency services standing by 24/7, ready to come to your aid. When the hurricane boils around you, His love keeps you on course, no matter how ferocious the winds howl, no matter how much water washes into the boat. God is on your side and will not only bring you into the eye of the storm, He will become the eye of your storm so that you may enjoy the "peace that passes all understanding." I would not be surprised if you looked around and found you already have His rescue team at work in your burning building. Often help stares us right in the face and we can't see it.

That was true for a Ground Zero rescue worker who was taking a well-deserved break. He was in the Respite Center near "the pile" and appeared agitated and worn out. Sitting at one of the tables, he held his head in his hands and rubbed his eyes with grimy fingertips, as if trying to erase the images the long hours had burned there. A female volunteer, one our church had sent, was serving coffee in the center and had noticed the agitated rescue worker, but hadn't approached him yet. Another rescue worker, one the volunteer had never seen before, suggested she "talk with that man over there."

She did and quickly found out that the rescue worker (we'll call him Dave) was in serious emotional trouble. A member of FDNY, he was deeply despondent. He'd found more than a dozen bodies of his fellow firefighters and was responsible for putting them in body bags and having them driven to the morgue. As the volunteer listened, she realized how sad he was and told him, "I'm a nurse and I understand how you're feeling."

"So you know the long hours," he managed, opening the door of communication just a crack.

"Very long hours," she said. "I worked in a trauma unit. Mostly with cancer patients."

Dave's eyes came up to hers. Even though they appeared worn and beaten, they managed to mirror the compassion he was being shown. He must have realized that he would be understood, but mostly that he'd be safe, because he relaxed appreciably and began to talk as if an old friend were listening. This rescue worker had stepped onto an important path in the man's healing.

Talking to sincere friends is one of the best ways to heal a broken heart. And no doctor's prescription is needed. Because the search-and-rescue teams were the ones who handled the dead, they ended up on "the pile" several times a week. The best mental-health medicine for these teams was to be debriefed after every call-out, give them the chance to just talk, get the bad out, and have it replaced by a friend's love and support.

It you're going through Ground Zero, you probably have people nearby whom God has sent. Who are they? They're people you know, who know the Lord, and are good listeners. Seek them out, then open up and let the floodgates of healing overflow your soul.

How many loving, compassionate friends has God brought to those affected by Ground Zero? A lot. If you just look at my experience alone, I spoke with chaplains from the FBI, ATF, DMORT, NYPD, Coast Guard,

U.S. Army, U.S. Navy, American Red Cross, Salvation Army, and numerous other agencies and organizations. In addition, we trained 500 local clergy in a ten-day period. God has brought a large army to help those touched by this horrific event.

Nothing refreshes and aids a sick man so much as the affection of his friends. (Seneca the Younger)

Let's review some spiritual resources available to rescue us in our time of grief.

First, never give up hope. Hope brings stability, a sense that no matter how rough the seas are now, there are calm waters ahead. And yes, you'll make it to those waters. Next, find the peace you seek by calling upon the name of Jesus, then let the peace that He promised fill your cup to overflowing. And as you let God's peace rule in your heart, turn your heart towards God and let His love begin His healing process in you.

Although you may be overwhelmed by your Ground Zero and it seems like life can never return to normal, trust God—you *will* recover. While you work through the healing process, remember that even though the storm rages all around you, there is always an eye you can work your way toward, where God's serenity reigns. Finally, an important element in the healing process is talking through the pain. Look around you, find someone nearby who will listen compassionately and who understands you.

. . . but we also glory in tribulations, knowing that tribulation produces perseverance; and perseverance, character; and character, hope. Now hope does not disappoint, because the love of God has been poured out in our hearts by the Holy Spirit who was given to us. (Rom. 5:3-5)

CHAPTER 8
LOVE

In this the love of God was manifested toward us, that God has sent His only begotten Son into the world, that we might live through Him.

1 John 4:9

F rancis Thompson (1859-1907) wrote a classic poem titled "The Hound of Heaven," a poem that reminds us that God, in some ways, is like a hunting dog. He has our scent and is determined to track us down. As I wrote this chapter, I thought about this title. You see, there are three dog stories I experienced at Ground Zero and I'd like to share them with you.

PERSISTENT LOVE

The first dog story is about the search-and-rescue dogs. My good friend Mickey Stonier is the chaplain for the San Diego Fire Department. They sent their search-and-rescue team to Ground Zero, and we met them there. San Diego has one of the finest programs in the country, and their search dogs are phenomenal at the jobs they do. Disaster dogs are trained for two major functions at a disaster site. The first is to find survivors. The rescue dogs arrive on the scene as soon as possible. The second job is to find bodies. Dogs trained for this work are called cadaver dogs. One might think the same dog could do both functions, but they're trained differently; so one specializes in rescue and the other in recovery. Over 300 dogs helped the NYPD search "the pile" in their 24/7 efforts.

Dogs with this special training are rare. Although the qualifications for a good dog are varied, all must possess exceptional agility, the ability to follow commands in chaotic situations, and the ability to overcome noisy distractions and their own innate fears. An exceptional dog can search about 10,000 square feet of rubble, and cadaver dogs can detect human remains the size of a common nail.

These dogs are committed to their work. They search with zeal and ignore the cuts and bruises they inevitably get. To keep them healthy, an animal mobile emergency unit remained near Ground Zero. It was staffed by veterinarians and equipped with all they would need. There was concern that because of the dust, smoke, and ashes in the air at Ground Zero these dogs might suffer aftereffects from breathing so much of it.

My former secretary and longtime friend, Beverly Stewart, sent me an amazing email about those dogs. While she watched television, as she saw the dogs at work combing the rubble at Ground Zero, she realized their paws were exposed to extreme conditions. And they were extreme. Firefighters' boots actually began melting when they stayed in one spot too long. She works for FedEx, so she made arrangements with a company who made dog booties to donate them and arranged for FedEx to fly them there free. It always amazes me how people are inspired to help in times of trouble. Beverly's action, like those of millions of other Americans, is not the reaction the terrorists expected from the people of our great land.

Dogs are loving, loyal, and wonderful companions. They also can be intimidating and fierce. I have seen dogs display all these elements while on patrol—and when they're intimidating and fierce, they're definitely equalizers for a lone patrol officer. I remember one warm summer evening in San Diego when the police were in hot pursuit of a stolen van. On the freeway, screaming along at high speed, we eased up behind it and immediately noticed a guy spray-painting the rear windows from the inside. It would turn out to be a real waste of his artistic abilities since in about ten minutes he'd be arrested and handcuffed, but at that moment he thought he was keeping some kind of secret from the increasing number of squad cars who were in pursuit. By the time the chase left the freeway for the surface streets, we had close to a dozen cars flashing behind us. San Diego, America's sixth largest city, is in a large county that borders Mexico. This van was stolen at the border, loaded up with 28 people who'd entered the United States illegally, and aimed north. When it was finally brought to a stop and the passengers were sitting on the ground, hands clasped behind their heads, I saw an interesting testimonial to a dog's ability to intimidate. It didn't take all of the police officers to oversee this group. When the K9 unit pulled up and the handler and his dog got out, the over two dozen people who sat on the ground became anxiously quiet. A few minutes later the other officers slid behind their steering wheels and drove off. They weren't needed. Not everyone who was under arrest spoke or understood English, but they all understood *dog*.

Both police officers and firefighters respect these highly trained animals. They bring calm reassurance to everyone deployed with them at a scene. The same was true at "the pile." But though they brought a sense of calm purpose everywhere they worked, Ground Zero wore deeply on them, too, since dogs are emotional creatures. It was particularly evident when there would be long spans of time between successful rescues or recoveries. The dogs were trained to find people, and when they didn't, they'd get depressed. Everyone could see their tails dragging, and their handlers could see the deep sadness and frustration in their eyes. To perk the dogs up, firefighters and police officers would hide in the rubble, then the handlers would send the dogs to find them. The moment they flushed one of the workers out, their tails would waggle with excitement and their eyes would glisten—they'd done what they were trained to do!

When our Ground Zero strikes, when our routine gets knocked off track, we get discouraged, become disorganized, get depressed. Will we ever get back to the way things were? Each of us has heard the wailings of a friend going through divorce: "I will never marry again!" A child being disciplined may cry out to the parent, "I hate you!" The parent may feel like the world has suddenly stopped spinning: "How could my child hate me?" When events unfold quickly we can become stunned, shocked that the situation has us in its sights. We try to process everything that's happening around us for instant clarification. But we go into overload and our sensors start flashing warning lights. Depression sets in, just like it did for these dogs. They had a life, and their life was structured around their responsibilities. They felt great satisfaction when they fulfilled them; they felt empty, useless, when they didn't.

STRENGTHENING LOVE

The Bible tells of a courageous prophet named Elijah. We don't know much about his background—his family, his upbringing. We do know he was a righteous man who loved and served God by taking His message to Israel. His bold, outspoken manner placed his life in danger many times. But at no time was it in greater danger than when he confronted King Ahab and Queen Jezebel with their wickedness. Jezebel wore the regal pants in the family, and the country knew it. They feared Jezebel. Nobody dared cross her—including Elijah, the prophet of God.

Elijah probably could have kept a reasonably low profile if it hadn't been for the fact that Jezebel had her own religion. She worshiped the pagan god

Baal, and she and her priests led the nation in Baal worship. God wasn't impressed by this activity and sent Elijah to Ahab and Jezebel to express His irritation. This showdown is described in 1 Kings 18, and what a showdown it was! Elijah told Ahab to bring all Israel to Mt. Carmel along with the 450 prophets of Baal and 400 prophets of Asherah (the Babylonian goddess of pleasure, sex, fortune, and happiness). These prophets were all honored with a place at Jezebel's table. She sponsored them. When everyone arrived, Elijah took command of the situation and told the crowd that God would show Himself mighty this day. He shouted out to the people, "How long will you falter between two opposing opinions? If the Lord is God, follow Him; but if Baal, follow him." Here is the story as told in the Scripture:

> *"Therefore let them give us two bulls; and let them choose one bull for themselves, cut it in pieces, and lay it on the wood, but put no fire under it; and I will prepare the other bull, and lay it on the wood, but put no fire under it.*
>
> *"Then you call on the name of your gods, and I will call on the name of the Lord; and the God who answers by fire, He is God." So all the people answered and said, "It is well spoken."*
>
> *Now Elijah said to the prophets of Baal, "Choose one bull for yourselves and prepare it first, for you are many; and call on the name of your god, but put no fire under it."*
>
> *So they took the bull which was given them, and they prepared it, and called on the name of Baal from morning even till noon, saying, "O Baal, Hear us!" But there was no voice; no one answered. And they leaped about the altar which they had made.*
>
> *And so it was, at noon, that Elijah mocked them and said, "Cry aloud, for he is a god; either he is meditating, or he is busy, or he is on a journey, or perhaps he is sleeping and must be awakened."*
>
> *So they cried aloud, and cut themselves, as was their custom, with knives and lances, until the blood gushed out on them.*
>
> *And it was so, when midday was past, that they prophesied until the time of the offering of the evening sacrifice. But there was no voice; no one answered, no one paid attention.*
>
> *Then Elijah said to all the people, "Come near to me." So all the people came near to him. And he repaired the altar of the Lord that was broken down.*

And Elijah took twelve stones, according to the number of the tribes of the sons of Jacob, to whom the word of the Lord had come, saying, "Israel shall be your name."

Then with the stones he built an altar in the name of the Lord; and he made a trench around the altar large enough to hold two seahs of seed.

And he put the wood in order, cut the bull in pieces, and laid it on the wood, and said, "Fill four waterpots with water, and pour it on the burnt sacrifice and on the wood."

Then he said, "Do it a second time," and they did it a second time; and he said, "Do it a third time," and they did it a third time.

So the water ran all around the altar; and he also filled the trench with water.

And it came to pass, at the time of the offering of the evening sacrifice, that Elijah the prophet came near and said, "Lord God of Abraham, Isaac, and Israel, let it be known this day that You are God in Israel, and that I am Your servant, and that I have done all these things at Your word.

"Hear me, O Lord, hear me, that this people may know that You are the Lord God, and that You have turned their hearts back to You again."

Then the fire of the Lord fell and consumed the burnt sacrifice, and the wood and the stones and the dust, and it licked up the water that was in the trench.

Now when all the people saw it, they fell on their faces; and they said, "The LORD, He is God! The LORD, He is God!"

(1 Kings 18:23-39)

An amazing story, isn't it? Elijah was fearless. He took complete control over the forces of evil, and God honored his faith and brought the fire down upon the bull Elijah had prepared. Elijah was a pretty gutsy guy. Nothing was going to twist his world around, right? Wrong! Following this showdown, Elijah had all of the false prophets executed, including the prophets that sat at Jezebel's table, whom she financed. Jezebel was so angry to be made the fool, she sent a messenger to Elijah threatening his life, telling him he'd be dead within twenty-four hours. What did Elijah do? He ran! And he didn't stop until he was a day's journey from the king and queen. Hiding himself in the wilderness, he cried out to God that he might die. "It is enough! Now, Lord, take my life, for I am no better than my fathers" (1 Kings 19:4).

Elijah had a classic case of depression. He'd worked hard and long, had faced harsh conditions and situations, battled wicked people and won. And now he was depressed. Drained of emotional energy, he fell asleep, only to be awakened by an angel who gave him food and water. After nourishing himself, he fell asleep again. The angel came a second time and told him to eat and drink again, "because the journey is too great for you."

Can't you see how this strong man fell apart when his world was challenged? He could take on nearly a thousand false prophets, but one woman forced him to run. When we are depressed, sleep is one of God's natural remedies. We need to sleep all we can, then do as the angel told Elijah. We need to eat balanced meals and drink lots of water. If Ground Zero can produce depression for specially trained dogs, and if one of the Bible's greatest characters can become depressed, it is very possible for you to have a bout of depression during stressful times.

When our critical-incident stress-management teams debrief dispatchers or law-enforcement officers after a major incident, we always have fresh fruit and vegetables handy, along with fresh, cool water. It may take up to two hours for everyone to say what needs to be said. In one high-school shooting we spent four hours with the county dispatchers on duty that day.

DISTRACTING LOVE

The second dog story is about two dogs that were used to bring comfort to me. I came across a man and a woman; their two dogs were lying on the ground in front of their bench. Both dogs wore vests. I asked the couple if I could help them in any way. As we talked I knelt and began patting the dogs and stroking their chins as I would with my two dogs. I was reminded of my dogs and how much they loved me to take them for a run in the park. The man explained they had just flown in from Portland, Oregon, and were looking for a place to serve. "I was born and raised in Portland," I said.

"We have these two compassion dogs and feel we could be of service to someone."

That roused my curiosity. "What's a compassion dog?"

The woman answered, "They're trained to just love people and let people love them." We take them to convalescent and children's hospitals and anyplace people need comfort and love."

I understood. And the longer I knelt there petting these precious animals, the more I understood. I found my stress evaporating, released by loving these two dogs. Before I said good-bye to them, I actually felt relaxed. I also felt God at work again. Before I *did* say goodbye, I told them about a few children's centers and the Family Assistance Center at Pier 92 that could use their help. As they thanked me they added, "Do you know how we could find someone who's working here at Ground Zero?"

I suggested the Red Cross or the Family Assistance Center or one of the FDNY or NYPD temporary headquarters nearby. "We were on the plane from Portland and the man sitting next to us told us when we get to New York to look for a man named Mike MacIntosh. He will help you."

"Are you joking?" I said, "I'm Mike MacIntosh!"

Those two travel-weary dogs taught me a great lesson. When you're worn out there's always enough time to take a break. It is important for us to get back to our old routines. Even if that routine contains a simple walk with your dog. When the rubble is stacked tangled and confusing in front of us, the very sight of it can be overwhelming. Staring up at all of that chaos of unfinished business can depress us. We need distractions of love to remind us that things will return to normal at some point in the future. You may discover that ultimately it's those little love-distractions of life that make your life worth living.

> *Then little children were brought to Him that He might put His hands on them and pray, but the disciples rebuked them.*
> *But Jesus said, "Let the little children come to Me, and do not forbid them; for of such is the kingdom of heaven." (Matt. 19:13-14)*

It is the childlike acceptance of life that can keep our hearts from desperation. Children are an example of the simplicity of heaven. Petting your dog or holding your cat can soothe the anxious heart. Walking on the beach or riding a bicycle with someone you love can fill your emotional lungs with clean, fresh air and revive your soul.

DETERMINED LOVE

The third dog story is about Roselle, a courageous, gentle, three-year-old golden Labrador. Roselle is a guide dog that serves Michael Hingson, who is blind. At least two guide dogs were in the Twin Towers on September

11th. Each was with its owner. Roselle hurried to Mr. Hingson's side when the first plane struck. "She knew something was different," he said. "But she never freaked out and never lost her focus." From the 78th floor, Roselle brought Michael Hingson down the stairwell step by step. Roselle would step down, then wait for Michael, then step down again and wait. Somewhere around the 25th floor someone was handing out bottles of water. Hingson and Roselle, who was panting heavily, stopped for the refreshment. Then they continued their descent, step by step. Approximately one hour after the plane hit, Roselle and her master walked safely from the building. I had the privilege of meeting Roselle and her owner, Michael Hingson, and his wife. We were together with Lisa Beamer (the widow of the courageous young man credited for helping stop a fourth airplane from crashing into another building) and others for a statewide memorial at the PNC Bank Arts Center in Holmdel, New Jersey.

As Roselle's master stood at the podium, she stood patiently next to his left leg. I was in a daze myself, having just finished eleven nonstop days of work in New York City. I couldn't help but focus on this dog and wonder what had been at work inside her that day that allowed her to bring her master down more than seventy stories in a burning building? How did she ignore all the distractions, all the noise and frantic people hurtling past her? She definitely had discipline for her job and devotion for her master.

Prior to this event we were backstage meeting various people involved with the program. I was pleased to see the large number of police and security personnel at the doors and with us backstage. So they would know who we were, we all had "Full Access" ID tags hanging around our necks. These tags allowed us to roam freely without the guards being too concerned. As I looked Roselle over, I realized that someone had put a chain with a "full access" stage pass around this heroic dog's neck too. It was good to know that Roselle's background check was spotless!

When you are facing a Ground Zero in your life, remember that God is the Hound of Heaven. He has your scent and He is going to find you and rescue you from any danger.

> *The fear of the LORD leads to life*
> *And he who has it will abide in satisfaction;*
> *He will not be visited with evil.* (Prov. 19:23)

L O V E

When your world falls apart, look around for help. As the shock subsides, make sure your hope is intact, and trust God that something good will result from this. Look for ways to survive the emotional roller coaster you may be on. Good food, plenty of sleep, and lots of water are a must. Don't forget the simple things in your daily routine that help stabilize you. And don't forget those dogs and cats and those other love-distractions you've come to rely on. They can bring tremendous comfort, and you'll begin to believe that your world will one day be as it was. Don't overlook these little ingredients; often they are the small spices that God uses to bring profound flavor to our lives. And never forget, God is lovingly working on your behalf through so many avenues, at so many different levels.

And finally, though you may not have a guide dog to steer you through the rubble, you do have something even greater. The Bible is the greatest guide available to all of us.

Psalm 119:105 says, "Your word is a lamp to my feet and a light to my path." Pick up a Bible today and read the Psalms. And as you do, discover the comfort and healing God has woven into them. King David wrote most of the Psalms during times of sadness and grief, deep depression and loneliness. He wrote them at the death of his children, after he had committed adultery, when his enemies were near to killing him, when his personal health had failed, and during many other devastating times in his long life— all of them more devastating than any I have ever faced. When you've learned to listen to God speak through the Psalms, move on to the Gospels and learn of Jesus' struggles against evil and see how He died for you. If He had only died for mankind we'd see Him as a martyr. But Jesus rose from the dead, then ascended to heaven with the promise He would return again to us one day. Many believe that the attack on the World Trade Center is a sign that His coming is soon.

Give God a chance to guide you to safety this very day. Simply say a prayer something like this:

Dear God,

I don't understand everything about You, but I want to ask You to help me.

My life is in pain as I see my world collapsing. Please come into my life and bring the peace of Your Son, Jesus, into my heart.

Help me, God! I need You to please help me.

Amen

CHAPTER 9
IDENTITY

I will praise You, for I am fearfully and wonderfully made;
Marvelous are Your works,
And that my soul knows very well.
My frame was not hidden from You,
When I was made in secret,
And skillfully wrought in the lowest parts of the earth.

Psalm 139:14-15

In the first few days following the September 11th tragedy, the National Guard Armory was a chaotic place to be. There were several National Guardsmen at the entrance to the armory along with NYPD officers standing on the steps and at the street level leading up to the steps. The number of people who were in motion at any given time inside that armory was at least six or seven dozen. With constant motion and constant talking going on in every square foot of this room, you couldn't help but feel the hustle and the bustle of the activity. But for all this activity—and it's hard *not* to remember every moment of it—there is a scene in particular I know I'll never forget. (Even as I write this, the memory of it is so vivid I can see it as clearly as I see this page before me, it was so packed with meaning.)

In the early part of any rescue effort, when there's still a chance people are alive, hopes and spirits run high. And both soar even higher when survivors are found, when they are returned from the missing to the arms of their loved ones. When that happened at Ground Zero, the whole nation cheered.

IDENTIFICATION

Even early on, a major job is identification of those who haven't survived—putting a name to the remains. And all too often, the remains are not easily identifiable; so extraordinary measures must be taken. There are a number of measures available: fingerprints, dental records, iris scans, handprints, blood samples, photographs, tattoos, birthmarks, and other markings. Recently a new method has jumped to the forefront: DNA fingerprinting (or typing). And because of its reliability, and because identification can be made from even small remains, it's become the method of choice.

So what is a DNA fingerprint? DNA stands for deoxyribonucleic acid. It's a genetic material formed into strands, or threads, in the cell nuclei of all living things. In mammals (like us), the strands of DNA are grouped into structures called chromosomes. With the exception of identical twins, the complete DNA of each individual is unique, just like fingerprints; thus the idea of a DNA fingerprint. So how do they lift this print? It's a little more complicated and takes a lot more time than just dusting for it. To create a DNA fingerprint, first the technician takes a DNA sample from the body tissue or fluid, like hair, blood, or saliva. Then, by using enzymes, the technician segments the DNA, and, using a process called electrophoresis, arranges the segments by size. Once arranged, they're marked with probes and exposed on X-ray film, where they form a pattern of black bars. This pattern is the DNA fingerprint. If the DNA fingerprints produced from two different samples match, it's virtually certain that the two samples came from the same person. (If researchers are able to get a complete DNA map from a sample, the odds are 1 in up to 30 billion that a duplicate sample exists.)

DNA fingerprinting was first used for identification purposes in 1985. Although it was originally used to detect genetic diseases, forensic scientists soon started using DNA fingerprints in criminal investigations. The first U.S. criminal conviction based on DNA evidence took place in 1988.

It's not hard to see that identifying remains using DNA takes a good amount of technician and laboratory time. Identifying thousands of remains, as was required at the World Trade Center, is a massive job. As those remains were slowly and painstakingly identified, several thousand people came in the course of a day to the armory to see if their loved ones were among those identified. Initially, though, most who came weren't aware DNA fingerprinting was being used. They were asked to come back with a comb or brush belonging to the missing loved one to help forensics. Returning with these items was hard and doing so sparked an emotional war inside thousands of anxious hearts. Each person knew that handing over the item would result in one of two outcomes: their loved one would be found to be still missing and possibly still alive in the pile, or their worst nightmare would be confirmed and they'd find out their loved one was dead.

IDENTITY

FACING THE WORST

The instant forensics started DNA fingerprinting, the stress level rose for the family members and friends, and it rose for the interviewing officers too. It's right that our sympathies are with those family and friends of the victims; often their loss is incalculable. But the wear on these interviewing officers was tremendous as well. It's for this reason that I've devoted so much of my free time to serving law enforcement. Even though they wear a uniform and carry a badge, they are real people with real lives and real families. And they are generally misunderstood. After speaking with several NYPD officers working in the great hall, I saw the impact this process had on them. They were in an ancient, drafty building and working long, agonizing hours dealing heartbeat to heartbeat with the distraught families of the victims of the most atrocious evil ever perpetrated in their city. Of course their natural instinct was to be outside at the site or around the city, combing the area for bad guys, following up leads, looking for clues. Obedience, patience, and compassion kept them at their posts.

When family members were asked to come back, we knew this was the time chaplains and clergy would be truly needed. Sure enough, when a police officer raised a hand, it signaled need for immediate spiritual care.

You see, when the hairbrush, comb, or toothbrush was handed to the police officer and put into an evidence container, the impact of what was happening fell on many like the proverbial ton of bricks. They knew the terrible truth the item might reveal, what was behind the request for these items: it was unlikely that their loved one was still alive. That's why so many handed these items over reluctantly, engaging in a short-lived tug-of-war before completely giving up control. For many, the moment their fingers let go signified the letting go of whatever hope they'd still been clinging to of seeing their father or mother or wife or sister again. Otherwise, why would forensics need a DNA sample? For many, the impact went beyond devastating. Parents and spouses fainted at the table, while some fell to the floor. Screams would rise up like sharp spikes, and loud sobbing would tear at us from every direction.

My heart broke over and over as I saw young families with one parent arrive, only to discover they would never see the other parent again, or I'd see children without parents leave knowing they'd be that way forever. Or I'd see people waiting alone—husbands, wives, brothers, sisters, aunts, uncles—the lines of despair went on and on. Upon hearing their news, some people would weep and tremble alone, while others clung to someone near-by for comfort. Some would just stare off somewhere confused, their heads moving almost imperceptibly from side to side, their very insides denying what they would soon inevitably have to face. Some were angry, others depressed, still others both angry and terrified. Every emotion you could imagine was represented somewhere—every emotion but joy. Being both a pastor and a chaplain, I focused on both sides of those tables—the devastation being visited upon the victim's family, and the law enforcement people delivering the horrific news. Although I comforted people when I could, I quickly found there was little to do but pray. This was a tragedy literally of biblical proportions, and it needed the God of the Bible to bring His healing and peace to this place.

KNOWN BY GOD

Jesus consistently reminded those listening how much God loved them. He was very candid about God's concern for all His creation, the human race being at the center of it, and at the center of His focus. Perhaps you think God is so far away He's out of touch with you. Not so. Jesus said, "And do not fear those who kill the body but cannot kill the soul. But rather fear Him which is able to destroy both soul and body in hell. Are not two sparrows sold for a copper coin? And not one of them falls to the ground apart from your Father's will. But the very hairs of your head are all numbered. Do not fear therefore; you are of more value than many sparrows" (Matt 10:28-31).

Think of it: "the very hairs of your head are all numbered"! When people left home September 11th for work, they left their hairbrushes and combs lying on the bathroom counter, each with DNA samples in the strands of their hair. God knew the exact number of hairs that remained on their heads. He was intimately involved with each of these victims the moment they woke up. He saw them shower, eat breakfast, and leave their homes. He knew their families would need comfort in the hours to come, so He prepared thousands of people, such as myself, to bring sympathy, comfort, and love to the tens of thousands suddenly plunged into those dark valleys of grief.

We often don't give God the credit He deserves. If He knows the strands of hair on our heads, He must be even more concerned with the larger issues facing us. Jesus mentioned sparrows being sold two for a penny in the marketplace. Imagine how insignificant that purchase would be for us today. It's nearly impossible to find anything we can buy today for a penny. In fact, it costs more to mint the penny than it's worth. Yet if God has His eye on the sparrows, no matter how little they're worth monetarily, how much more will He have His eye on us, the crown of His creation!

How do you want to be identified today? Identity is not about credentials or DNA. It's about who you are. People identify themselves today with music, money, education, clothes, popularity, and so many other categories. Teenagers, if left to their own devices, generally allow their identities to be shaped by peers, the music they listen to, the television shows and movies they watch. We adults often identify ourselves with our occupations, or the groups of people with which we associate. A Madison Avenue executive doesn't identify with a motorcycle club. Unless, of course, he's on his Harley on the weekends—and if he is, on Monday he's an "ad guy," and on Saturday, he's in "Hog heaven."

We associate and identify with people we respect, who share our values and interests, who dress like us, listen to the music that we like, frequent the same places we do. Our identities are important to us, and we work hard most of our lives shaping them. But when we break out of careers and weekends and begin to talk about life, death, and eternal issues, it's important to have the right identity—a heavenly identity. If our identity is associated with the things of earth, we know for certain they will pass away when the earth passes away. However, if our identity is with heavenly values, if our names are written there, we know for certain our identities, our names, will never pass away.

If anything has sprouted from the ashes of the September 11th tragedy, it's that we, as a nation, have faced the reality of life and death. The nation of our parents faced it in the Korean conflict and World War II, our grandparents in World War I, and our great-grandparents arrived at an awareness of their own mortality at Shiloh, and Gettysburg, and the Wilderness during the Civil War. Individually we all know we're going to die one day; we've faced it. But as a nation, we are now a generation who stands hand in hand facing a reality that most, until then, hid from: we are all going to die someday. If it's from terrorism or simply old age, no matter how it happens, the fact remains that we are going to die. So it becomes extremely important that any identity crisis we may have be faced eye to eye and taken care of.

IDENTITY IN CHRIST

Paul probably wrote more about life in Christ than any of the other New Testament writers. The term "in Christ" is found in seventy-six different locations in the New Testament, and most were penned by Paul.

> *There is therefore now no condemnation to those who are in Christ Jesus, who do not walk according to the flesh, but according to the Spirit. For the law of the Spirit of life in Christ Jesus has made me free from the law of sin and death* (Rom. 8:1-2)

If we are in Christ we now have the Spirit of life within us. This is the Spirit who raised Jesus from the dead. If our identity is with Jesus, then we know that we will have the eternal life He spoke of. While Jesus was in the Garden of Gethsemane he prayed that God would help the believers:

> *And the glory which You gave Me I have given them, that they may be one just as We are one: I in them, and You in Me; that they may be made perfect in one, and that the world may know that You have sent Me, and have loved them as You have loved Me.* (John 17:22-23)

Jesus wants us to be one with Him and the Father. What an identity that is for us to claim!

We have heard hundreds of reports of people praying and sharing their faith during the 9/11 disaster and in the rescue effort. Over and over again God has revealed His identity to rescue workers, volunteers, law enforcement personnel, firefighters, military personnel, and political people during these trying times during and since September 11th.

Notice in the text that follows, Paul reassures the believers that nothing—not even death—can separate us from the love of God in Christ Jesus. And if we identify with Him in this life, He watches over us and protects us from the devil himself.

> *For I am persuaded, that neither death nor life, nor angels nor principalities nor powers, nor things present nor things to come, nor height nor depth, nor any other created thing, shall be able to separate us from the love of God which is in Christ Jesus our Lord"* (Rom. 8:38-39)

To the Christian community in the beautiful city of Ephesus, Paul reaffirms that because their position and identity are in Christ, God blesses them with all of heaven's spiritual blessings. "Blessed be the God and Father of our Lord Jesus Christ, who has blessed us with every spiritual blessing in heavenly places in Christ" (Eph 1:3).

Finally, in his letter to the Philippian church the apostle reminds us that there are rewards for identifying with Jesus. Not only that, he reminds the readers that to be in Christ Jesus is actually a high calling. "I press toward the goal for the prize of the upward call of God in Christ Jesus" (Phil 3:14).

Many years ago a man called me about three in the morning and wanted me to bail him out of jail. With a large congregation, it's impossible for me to know everyone. So I asked him which of the assistant pastors were his friends, which home fellowship he belonged to, what ministry in the church was he serving in. His response was negative to all, so I figured he'd just been a casual visitor. I asked him why was he arrested. "I was arrested by two policemen in front of a sporting goods store. I'd broken the window of the display areas and climbed in."

Now interested, I asked, "Why did you break the window and jump inside the display area?"

"Well," he said, "I needed to get the crossbow."

"Crossbow? Why?"

"It was the demons," he said.

"What demons?"

"I took LSD a couple of hours earlier and I started hearing and seeing demons. They said they were going to kill me, so I had to get the crossbow to defend myself."

"You're probably still under the influence of the LSD and you can't get out until you speak with a lawyer, is that correct?"

"Yes, that's correct."

So I told him to do as the policemen told him, get some sleep to let the drugs wear off and call me later in the day. Unfortunately this young man chose to be identified with the world and not to take a higher calling and live a spiritual life for the glory of God—and be identified as being *in Jesus Christ*. Like so many others this man chose the downhill road. Why? Because you can coast. Coasting through life may be easy, but the dividends do not pay off in the end.

KNOWING WHO YOU ARE

As I look on my life, and then at the lives of my children (who are all grown), I notice each generation has its own music. Then the music brings with it that generation's own language and slang. The clothing industry surges in with a new craze because fads grow out of cultural change.

Take the music of the thirties and forties. People congregated to dance and have fun to the big band sound. Swing was the step of the day where upbeat couples held hands. Next came the crooners to steal the people's hearts. Frank Sinatra and Bing Crosby ruled the airwaves. The dance was now slow and close together, couples holding each other. Then "the king" arrived, and Elvis launched rock and roll. The hips began to swivel and the dance step was standing apart and moving rhythmically fast. By the time the Beatles broke into the spotlight on Ed Sullivan, dance was a little bit of everything. In recent years punk, heavy metal, and grunge music took the focus away from dancing and turned to head-banging, mosh pits, and piercings. Each generation had its own hair and clothing styles to fit the music. Generational identities were established, and at the same time cultural identities appeared. For Elvis we had the "war babies," for the Beatles it was the Baby Boomers, for Hootie and the Blowfish it was Generation X. Identity is big in so many ways, from designer clothes to brand-name wristwatches. It is big business. But when you identify who you are, it's more than big business, it's serious business.

In times of crisis be sure to maintain your identity. Don't turn to drugs, alcohol, or other uppers and downers to mask your hurt. Be honest with yourself and know that the ability to make it through depends on your making the right decisions. If your identity is found in God, then you will make it through your Ground Zero. Why? Because the God of the universe, the reservoir of all knowledge and wisdom, is walking right there with you, helping you make those decisions.

I am sure you're aware there is a book in heaven that is chock full of names. I call it the Who's Who of Heaven. It's also called the Lamb's Book of Life. The apostle John describes it this way:

> *And I saw the dead, small and great, standing before God, and books were opened. And another book was opened, which is the Book of Life. . . . And anyone not found written in the Book of Life was cast into the lake of fire.* (Rev. 20:12, 15)

Everyone whose name is written in that book can enter into the kingdom of heaven. On the other hand, everyone whose name is not written in this book cannot. This is the book that identifies God's children and, by inference, the devil's children. You may say, "Wait a minute! What do you mean by the devil's children?"

Listen to the dialogue between Jesus Christ and the religious leaders of His day. The religious leaders knew religion and how to keep the law, but they didn't know God and His grace. They felt because their bloodlines went back to Abraham they were safe. Their identity was with a man, not with the God who made the man, nor the God whom the man worshiped and adored. Basically that is religion as simply as can be described. God is not about religion, but about relationship.

> *Jesus said to them, "If God were your Father, you would love Me, for I proceeded forth and came from God; nor have I come of Myself, but He sent Me.*
>
> *"Why do you not understand My speech? Because you are not able to listen to My word.*
>
> *"You are of your father the devil, and the desires of your father you want to do. He was a murderer from the beginning, and does not stand in the truth, because there is no truth in him. When he speaks a lie, he speaks from his own resources, for he is a liar and the father of it.*
>
> *"But because I tell the truth, you do not believe me.* (John 8:42-45)

Do you want to have your name in the Lamb's Book of Life? Is that where you want to get your identity from? If you want to identify with the world and the devil, then your rewards will be for taking life's low road, for coasting and taking shortcuts. If you want to be rewarded because you chose the high road *in Christ Jesus,* then your name will be found in the Lamb's Book of Life,—the Who's Who of Heaven.

Never forget that every hair on your head is numbered, which should remind you that God knows your genes and your chromosomes and your DNA. He wants to help you and He wants to be the one who will rescue you and take you through your Ground Zero. If you want to identify with Him, He surely wants to identify with you. And as Jesus prayed, may you be one with God, as He is.

If you are not sure if your name is written in the Lamb's Book of Life, simply say this prayer:

Dear God, Please forgive me this day of my sins.

I want to have Your identity and to have Your Holy Spirit fill me with eternal life.

I pray that You will help me in my time of need. I ask that Jesus would come into my life and make me one with You, dear Father. And please, write my name in Your Book of Life.

In Jesus' name I ask these things.

Amen.

Your eyes saw my substance, being yet unformed.
And in Your book they were all written,
The days fashioned for me,
When as yet there were none of them.
(Psalm 139:16, (KJV)

CHAPTER 10
FREEDOM

*Therefore if the Son makes you free, you shall be free
indeed.*

John 8:36

W hile I waited at home for my flight to New York City, I (like everyone in the country) had the news channels on and I sat there glued to them.
If I had to leave, even for a moment, whatever I missed, my wife, Sandy,
who watched with me, brought me up to date when I got back. In the early
days of the tragedy, the scenes that truly touched me were of families and
friends lining the New York streets holding up and waving photographs of
their missing loved ones. The whole world watched with a collective sorrow
as hundreds were pulled from the crowds to tell reporters the heart-wrenching stories about their missing and lost. But as profound as watching it on
television was, walking among these people right there on the New York
concrete touched the very core of my heart and brought far deeper insights
into their unfathomable experience, an experience I could only witness from
the margins.

WALLS OF SORROW

My first encounter with these photographs and the people holding them
was outside the National Guard Armory on 26th and Lexington. Thousands
milled on the streets and sidewalks, while hundreds more stood in the lines
that wrapped around the building. Those in lines were waiting to get inside
to speak with an official about their missing loved ones. Plastered on both
sides of the entrance to this massive citadel were thousands of 8 x 11 photographs. They were everywhere I looked—photos of young secretaries,
stockbrokers, security guards, parents, grandparents, black, white, Asian,
every ethnic group, every color, every imaginable dress, hairstyle, look,
some smiling, some stern, some disinterested. None of them thinking these
snapshots would ever be taped to a wall by those they love, anxious for their
safety. When I saw those pictures and realized that real, flesh-and-blood peo-

ple were represented by each one of them—people with hopes, dreams, worries, people who loved and planned, genuine people, who were now gone because of the senseless act of terrorism—September 11th became very real to me. I didn't anticipate how these pictures in the next three days would have a profound impact on me for the rest of my life.

Chaplain Mindy Russel from the Sacramento Police Department and Chaplain Joseph Prudomme from the Fairfield (California) Police Department arrived on a military flight two days before I got there. They began the screening process for clergy and worked around the clock their first two days at the Family Assistance Center. Without their strong commitment to serve hurting families, I don't think the foundation of the Spiritual Care Unit would have been as solid as it was. As Mindy and Joseph continued their responsibilities, I took care of debriefing and assigning people to specific tasks in the armory. It took about three days for me to know the spiritual-care "hot spots," places within the armory where people who needed spiritual help could generally be found. One of those spots was in the basement.

After entering the building, the staircase to the basement was on the right. It was one of those wide staircases with the handrail down the center. People could walk two, maybe even three abreast down the twenty or so stairs. After the first few days hundreds of people filed down those stairs in seemingly endless lines to check on the whereabouts of their missing loved ones. This was a separate activity from the tables upstairs on the main floor. Upstairs the interviews took place and missing person reports were filled out. Downstairs was the list of known survivors. While they were in this line they would post their loved ones' pictures on the stairwell walls or on the walls that reached around the corner or on walls leading to the restrooms and past the restrooms to the room at the far end of the hall. Only God can give me the words here for you to feel the impact of what I came to call the Walls of Sorrow.

The pictures seemed to appear overnight. One person probably taped a photo to the wall, and immediately someone else did the same, and before long the wall was covered. The first time I became aware of the wall, I was working my way through the crowds figuring out the best way to help whomever was there. Then I saw it—and became quickly overwhelmed. To see the pictures taped everywhere in New York City and see them being held by people on the streets was one thing, but to stand in the midst of the family and friends who originated the photos was something beyond words.

And as they waited, they talked—a deep growl that filled old cavernous hallways, a subdued roar that charged the heavy air with electricity. Although brought together because of an unspeakable sadness, they were also bound to each other by that same sadness, and conversed like hundreds of old friends who'd just met at a class reunion. Such a special group, and now all of them able to talk with others who understood exactly what they were going through—understood their feelings, their grief, their fears, their rage. And for all the rage that had to be next to those walls, I sensed hope in the air as well.

The Past's Powerful Presence

I also sensed a definite presence the farther the line went down the stairs into the main hallway. The only other time I felt this telltale presence was during my visits to the Vietnam Veteran's Memorial Wall in Washington, D.C. "The Wall" isn't a *war* memorial but a *people* memorial—a memorial to those who are missing in action or were killed in Vietnam. There are 58,226 names carved into that wall, approximately 1,300 of them still missing. There were four criteria used in the memorial's design. It was to be reflective and contemplative in character, harmonize with its surroundings, contain the names of those who had died in the conflict or who were still missing, and make no political statement about the war. It succeeds on all counts and brings tears to my eyes whenever I visit it.

Standing in the armory basement early in the morning stillness or after midnight when the public was gone, I was affected the same way as I stood looking at the Walls of Sorrow—it took only a few moments for tears to begin filling my eyes. The presence of the Vietnam Veteran's Memorial was what I felt here. I certainly experienced the same sense of awe and humility and brokenness in both places. And when I emerge from the other side, when I leave the presence of such respect for those who've died, I'm speechless. It has dawned on me that the criteria for the Washington D.C. memorial is the same as the unspoken criteria used for this basement memorial. When we enter this stairwell and hallway we're immediately reflective and contemplative. The armory's age and architecture reflect the streets of New York, and posting these pictures spontaneously harmonizes with the surroundings. Every poster contained the name of a missing loved one. Finally, there were no political references at all. The similarities are striking between the Vietnam Veteran's Memorial (which, by the way cost $9,000,000 to build in

1982) and the simple, unplanned memorial in the basement of a National Guard Armory in New York City, created a few days after 9/11/01.

Unlike the Vietnam Memorial, we see pictures of the missing. And as we look at them, our hearts break. Even though I live in San Diego, the opposite corner of the country, these people are my neighbors, and your neighbors too. We know that almost three thousand of those neighbors died on that day, but standing there in front of those pictures, I saw no statistic. These were people, in spite of their ages, all in the prime of their lives. There was a grandfather, his granddaughter perched on his lap before the family Christmas tree. Others were serious pictures, others were funny; some were posed, others were action shots—probably taken on vacation, when all was smiles and laughter. Some pictures were unusual, like the one of an over-sixty gentleman in a business suit who stood beside an elephant. I wish I'd met him. I can only imagine his great sense of humor and adventure, and how beloved he must have been for his family to portray him in this fun-loving way.

On the Internet, I found a list of those named on the Vietnam Memorial in Washington D.C. With each name is a number—a number that indicates the location of the name etched on the black granite wall. Here's how the information on the web looks if you were looking for the names or photos of people killed in Vietnam:

> *Lt. Col. Annie Ruth Graham - On the Wall at 48W 012*
> *Chief Nurse at 91st Evac. Hospital, Tuy Hoa. From Efland, NC,*
> *she suffered a stroke in August 14, 1968 and was evacuated to Japan*
> *where she died four days later. A veteran of both World War II and*
> *Korea, she was 52.*

When the Family Assistance Center moved out of the armory to the pier, I met with the commanding officer of the armory and explained the impact the Walls of Sorrow had had on me. I wanted permission to bring a film crew from CNN into the basement to see this powerful display of love that had remained relatively unseen.

One of the CNN producers had interviewed me and we'd kept in touch via cell phones, as I helped her make other newsworthy contacts. The armory commander and the CNN crew both agreed the Walls of Sorrow were unique. The last I heard, a shrine of some sort would be left in the basement to honor the dead, the missing, and those who loved them enough to tape their pictures to the wall.

When the armory was alive with people, we always made sure we had chaplains and clergy in this hallway. And about every thirty minutes they'd break from their duties there and check both restrooms. They did this for good reason: they often found people sitting knees up on the floor, heads in their hands, weeping in profound, soul-cleansing sobs.

The Walls of Sorrow have been seared into my mind forever.

Our minds are like those walls. Instead of pictures, we've adorned them with memories. While some of those memories bring smiles, more often than we'd like they're framed with pain, and hung with hurt and trembling fingers. Then, as our beloved countrymen did, we stand in line again and again, studying the pictures and vital statistics and reviewing the biographies of our past. These infrequent strolls down "memory lane"—triggered by a certain song, a familiar fragrance, or when we visit a special place—can be wonderful moments, renewing and refreshing.

It's when we peer into that painful past, when we walk down our own Walls of Sorrow, that yesterday's agony returns.

THE DANGERS OF NOSTALGIA

But just as our good memories can be better than they really were (picnics of yesteryear seldom have ants), so can the painful memories play tricks on you. Often you don't remember things as they really were; memories distort the truth. And lingering too long with these memories—whether positive or negative—can become a type of bondage.

As the children of Israel struggled through the desert toward the Promised Land, they would often forget that God was protecting and leading them. They mumbled and grumbled about their hardships, especially the lack of food and water. They even went so far as to proclaim that they had been better off in Egypt, under Pharaoh's whip, than they were in the desert under God's protective wing. And as they walked, "groupies" (in Exodus they're called the "mixed multitude") followed along. These folks were neither committed to God nor to the children of Israel. They were tagalongs, hangers-on, just along for the ride—not the kind of people we want in our lives, and certainly not the people we want to have any influence on us.

The children of Israel complained that God didn't provide food well enough for them in this wilderness. Up to that point, He'd given them manna to eat each day (a wafer or muffin with coriander seed). In one passage of

Scripture it is called angel's food. So when God became weary of their constant demand for meat, he sent them quail to eat—a lot of quail—so many quail that the people, unrestrained, ate so much they made themselves sick. Here is how they responded to God's love and provision:

> *Now the mixed multitude who were among them yielded to intense craving; so the children of Israel also wept again and said: "Who will give us meat to eat? We remember the fish which we ate freely in Egypt, the cucumbers, the melons, the leeks, the onions, and the garlic; but now our whole being is dried up; there is nothing at all except this manna before our eyes!* (Num. 11:4-6)

As they spoke, the children of Israel walked before their own "walls of sorrow." Notice how their own tongues revealed how genuinely deceived they were. As Jesus said, "For out of the abundance of the heart the mouth speaks" (Matt. 12:34). Boy, did their lips reveal their empty hearts and shallow lives! First, they were influenced by the mixed multitude who couldn't control their own fleshly lusts. Then, when studying their own wall of memories, they touched up the pictures plastered there. They forgot being scourged by whips and controlled by brutality, their lives the property of a tyrannical pharaoh. Their memories blotted out his rage and how he forced them to make bricks for his buildings, in the end without providing straw. The Israelites were missing a broad chunk of reality, weren't they? Take note that they said, "our whole being is dried up," which clearly tells us that their being consisted of keeping the flesh alive. It's dangerous to focus solely on our flesh; it's also a waste of our time. Life in Egypt was a lot more complex and complicated than they seemed to want to remember.

Ezekiel, an Old Testament prophet, saw real "walls of sorrow" firsthand. Israel had involved themselves in intense idol worship, an abomination to God. Such worship hardened their hearts towards God's leading, and their desire to please God had vanished. Their priests had failed them. Instead of keeping the people focused on God, they led them way from Him. In an effort to bring His people back, God calls Ezekiel. But before He sends Ezekiel out, He first shows him what's truly happening within Israel, behind the people's backs.

Furthermore He said to me, "Son of man, do you see what they are doing, the great abominations that the house of Israel commits here, to make Me go far away from My sanctuary? Now turn again, you will see greater abominations."

So He brought me to the door of the court; and when I looked, there was a hole in the wall.

Then He said to me, "Son of man, dig into the wall"; and when I dug into the wall, there was a door.

And He said to me, "Go in, and see the wicked abominations which they are doing there."

So I went in and saw, and there—every sort of creeping thing, abominable beasts, and all the idols of the house of Israel, portrayed all around on the walls.

And there stood before them seventy men of the elders of the house of Israel, and in their midst stood Jaazaniah the son of Shaphan. Each man had a censer in his hand, and a thick cloud of incense went up.

Then He said to me, "Son of man, have you seen what the elders of the house of Israel do in the dark, every man in the room of his idols? For they say, 'The Lord does not see us, the Lord has forsaken the land.'" (Ezek. 8:6-12)

This particular scene had to break Ezekiel's heart. Here were the leaders of his country living dual lives, one public, one in the backrooms, out of the people's sight. But not out of God's. And what a powerful image for God to reveal to Ezekiel, the inner workings of a hideous idolatry inside His holy place; what would be equivalent to pornographic images hanging on your church walls today. How picturesque for us to read, "every man in the room of his idols." I'd like to make a connection between this wall of idols and the "Walls of Sorrow" I saw at Ground Zero.

FREEDOM FROM THE PAST

The mind is a powerful storage medium. In a way it's like a computer hard drive, which can contain volumes of information. And like a hard drive, the storage capacity seems unlimited, as does its ability to store and retrieve images, ideas, questions, answers, data, photos (still and moving), just about anything.

If you're in the midst of a Ground Zero, you also have a remembrance "wall" of images. Because a personal Ground Zero usually involves some significant loss, your memories—even the pleasant ones—are tinged with sorrow as you realize you will never experience them again. But please realize, your "wall of sorrows" can become a "wall of joy." We all have painful memories, that, when revisited, can cause considerable discomfort; but for all the discomfort, they don't need to control us, not now, not in the future. All our failures and mistakes can be blueprints to help us do better and rise above them.

To pass before the "Walls of Sorrow" was something I did for a week or so. In that sense it was a once-in-a-lifetime experience for me. But if I were to go there every day, to throw open the huge doors of that cavernous armory every day, and step down the stairs and stare at the memories of others every day, would be to put myself in bondage to the past. Living in the past, continuing to dwell on what might have been, would keep me from enjoying the life God has given me. I could never be free to learn something new, go on a great skiing vacation, climb a mountain, write a book, enjoy a good meal with friends, go to a movie with my wife. I'd be imprisoned by the past. I would never grow as a person, as a Christian. I would never mature in relationships. I could never accomplish anything new again because my mind would be constantly blazing the memories of that horrific day of loss.

The apostle Paul gives us some help here in our time of crisis: "Let this mind be in you which was also in Christ Jesus" (Phil. 2:5).

The New Testament is full of the words, thoughts, ideas, actions and interactions of Jesus Christ. If you were to spend some time just reading the Gospel according to Mark you would see that Jesus was consumed with two things—loving and serving people, and loving and serving God (unlike the children of Israel in the time of Moses, who were intent on serving themselves). What an encouragement to us—to think like Jesus, to allow His thoughts to become our thoughts. It will not only allow us to take down some of the posters and free up some wall space, it will allow us to learn of God's great love when our world is falling apart. When we see how Jesus worked with people when they were in crisis, we learn how to act during *our* times of crisis, we learn to trust God through it all.

Then we can begin to move out of our bondage to our Walls of Sorrow into the life of freedom that Jesus has for us.

CHAPTER 11
HOPE

Now may the God of hope fill you with all joy and peace in believing,
that you may abound in hope by the power of the Holy Spirit.

Romans 15:13

At the end of the hall in the basement of the National Guard Armory is a large room, probably large enough to seat more than fifty people theater style. But you didn't sit theater style; instead, folding tables were set up side by side facing the door with police officers sitting behind them. If you entered via the line that led through the "Walls of Sorrow" (described in the last chapter), these officers were the main attraction. In front of the officers were the lists of the collapse survivors, those found and transported to a local area hospital. Hundreds of people lined up each day—and we're talking about a long line. It led up the stairs to the armory, past the security barricades on the street, past the police and National Guard soldiers on the entrance steps, through the doorway, around the corner, and down the stairwell past the "Walls of Sorrow," and ultimately into this room. And each person in line held photos and the posters of loved ones clutched to their chests. During the hours they waited, as they moved slowly along, they pasted those pictures and posters everywhere they found an empty space.

THE ROOM OF LOST HOPE

We all knew the simple, obvious truth, but sometimes it was hard to face. You see, if the person you sought had been rescued and taken to a local hospital, the hospital staff or the police would have already notified you. In those first days following September 11th, hope in that line ran rampant. However, hope quickly vanished when you stepped up to a table, gave your loved one's name, and were told the person was still missing. The hope-balloon instantly popped. What started as a "line of hope," usually ended in a "room of lost hope." And the way the people left that room reflected their lost hope. Expectation turned to anxiety and tears, a measured cheer turned to clinging to friends they'd brought for support. Watching it was agonizing, so very agonizing.

No one knew better than I the support the family and friends of the victims needed. Sympathetic to those needs, we made sure counselors and clergy were available night and day for them. We placed chaplains near the entrance to the room and, as I mentioned, had them regularly check the restrooms. The chaplains were all volunteers, away from regular jobs and ministries. All were also tremendously skilled in serving people in pain.

I, on the other hand, found myself focused on the emotional needs of the law enforcement folks, those working behind the tables. Each one of them knew their ultimate job was to bring bad news, to dash hopes. Having to constantly look up into expectant eyes to see their words bring sudden, frightened desperation, takes a toll, and over time—over a short time, actually— hurts deeply. I tried as often as I could to drop into that room with a smile, handshake, word of encouragement, and a strong cup of black coffee for one or more of the dozen officers working there.

I often think about that room even now. I see its muted lighting, the exhausted personnel working behind the tables. I hear the noise in the hallway that actually quieted the closer people got to the door. I re-experience the devastated expressions of those leaving the room, reminding us how severe matters really were.

OTHER ROOMS OF LOST HOPE

When this room comes to mind I think of parallels to all the "rooms of lost hope" we enter during our lifetimes. There are a lot of them. And if we identify them we can help understand some of the problems they bring with them. Then, once we see them for what they are, we can receive the peace that releases us from our pain. What helps bring this peace? Someone there, when you come out of your "room of lost hope," to take your hand, to listen, or to simply love you and minister to you. Without this kind of support, you may never recover fully.

I was only fifteen years old when my oldest brother, David, died. I can remember so clearly his best friend's wife telling me he'd had an automobile accident. And what an accident. He was a passenger in a car going 70 miles per hour that hit a telephone pole. I don't remember the car, but I do remember every detail of the night my beautiful mother, Ruth, and I walked into the mortuary to view his open coffin. When I saw his body lying there clothed in his blue blazer, white shirt, and necktie, it seemed like a joke. He looked like he always did—he even had his famous smile. David had a great sense of humor and was a classic practical joker. I half expected him to leap off the white satin at any minute, point at us, and laugh. But, of course, he didn't. This wasn't a joke; this was a very harsh reality. Now, so many years later, a parent myself, I can only imagine the terrible knot of feelings my mother must have experienced as she stood there beside me, viewing the lifeless body of her oldest son.

How completely different the world would be today if there had been a chaplain or pastor standing outside that "room of lost hope." David was twenty-six years old, married, father of an eighteen-month-old boy, working for an airline at the Sacramento Airport as an assistant station manager, and, as if he didn't have enough to do, attending college. Acres of personality, quick-witted and intelligent, his life stretched out before him. I knew he could become anything he chose. I saw him as a man on a white charger. He was my hero, the first MacIntosh to go to college, our family's hope (he was our ticket out of our situation in Portland, Oregon) and my personal hope. I was sure my future would hold better things because of him. But that night, that very hot, sticky August night, my hope was crushed. I needed—my life needed—someone with comforting words, someone who would speak living spiritual truth, outside that "room of lost hope." My mother needed someone there too. Someone who understood her grief, someone to wrap comforting arms around her and let her cry. Unfortunately, no one was there.

On the way back to our motel room, we pulled up to a stoplight. The haunting, melancholy strains of Santo and Johnny's "Sleepwalk" played on the radio. To this day when I hear that song on a golden-oldies station, my heart reaches back to August 19, 1959. As we sat at the light, a Chevy pulled up next to us. In it were four teenage boys laughing loudly, poking at each other boisterously. One of them sobered and glanced over at me. He gave me one of those narrow-eyed tough-guy looks. My blood spiked hot and I suddenly wanted to jump out of the car and take on all four of them. My mother had no idea what I was thinking. Had she, she might have yanked out some of the seeds of anger and resentment my brother's tragic death planted in my young, tender heart. Over the next few years these seeds sank deep roots, and the resulting anger grew like a gathering storm, a storm that took on a ferocious energy as the enemy of my soul fed it through adolescence and young adulthood. As I waded through the swamp of those years, I never knew why I was always getting into fights, or why I quit high school in my senior year. If only I had had someone waiting outside that mortuary door where I'd lost all hope, my world would never have fallen apart.

HOPE IS POSSIBLE

Maybe you, too, left your own "room of lost hope" with your life in tangles. May I share something with you that it's taken me forty-three years to learn? Someone *was* standing outside that mortuary, and He *was* waiting to wrap comforting arms around my mother and me. His arms were outstretched, empathetic tears moistened His eyes, and He was bursting with compassion and mercy for us. The problem was, we didn't notice Him. He was there with us at the mortuary the next day, as well. He even went to the graveside services, where David was honored with a twenty-one-gun salute, and the American flag, taken from his coffin, was folded and presented to David's wife. He stood right behind where mom, Kent, and I sat, yet we didn't see Him there, either. We might have looked for Him had we known how important He was. But we didn't. His name is Jesus Christ and He wanted to talk to us, but we weren't ready. He was standing outside your "room of lost hope" too. In fact, He was in there with you. He was ready to comfort you then, and He's near you now, ready to be everything you need Him to be.

My father died at the age of eighty-three. He was an alcoholic and lived a withdrawn alcoholic's life. His sister and her husband were also alcoholics; his father, William, was from Salt Coates, Scotland, and he, too, was an alcoholic. I came from a "drinking family." On the flipside of that coin, my mother was a nondrinker. My great-grandmother Lane was from Ireland and lived in Portland, Oregon. She was a strong supporter and leader of the now extinct WCTU (Women's Christian Temperance Union). Grandma Lane would take my mom with her to the meetings, where her little, curly-haired, ten-year-old granddaughter would sing a song and speak out against the evils of "demon rum." I took after my father's side of the family and began drinking at fifteen; my first beer was two months after my brother's death. In the next eleven years I crossed the thresholds of so many bars, taverns, clubs, and "dance halls," I could never have counted them all. Each was a "room of lost hope."

How many people have ruined lives because of rooms filled with alcohol or drugs? They go into them to "have a good time" or to "party" or they're looking for "Mr. Right" or the "girl of their dreams." And they come out of those rooms filled with emptiness and dissatisfaction. Some of these rooms are full of neon and leather booths, or bars with leather stools, pool tables, big screens, live music, or a DJ. They're designed for one purpose—to sell alcohol and make money. The devil's with you in these rooms, and he has an agenda of his own: sell alcohol, make money, and drain the patrons of all hope. Maybe you or your loved one has entered these places and left these "rooms of lost hope" in despair.

In most cities, the police start watching the busiest bars around 2 A.M. They know that's the time drunks start climbing into cars and terrorizing the nearby highways and byways. Although the drunks don't like it, quite often the police are removing these risky drivers before they do real damage.

In the same manner, Jesus Christ stands outside these places with arms wide open ready to accept anyone coming out without hope. If drinking or drug use is draining you and your family of the little bit of hope you still have, turn toward God right now and take His amazing cure. If you're prone to visit those "rooms of lost hope" frequently, it's time for you to leave them behind and begin a new life.

The stockbroker's office or the Internal Revenue's offices or your accountant's office can also be for you a "room of lost hope." You carry your box of cancelled checks, bank statements, and pertinent files with you, and before you know it the person on the other side of the desk tells you you've hit bottom—you're bankrupt. Only God knows how many have entered this particular "room of lost hope," but, if the statistics are right, it's got to be a bunch. In America from 1990 thru 1995 there were 5,333,096 bankruptcies. From 1996 thru 2001, the number was up to 8,090,287. That's 13,423,383 bankruptcies. That tells me, and it should tell you, that if you are suffering a financial Ground Zero, you're not alone in your despair. But even though you've got company with you as you are leaving that room, it's still easy to have no hope for your financial future. In all of the rooms you've entered and left over your lifetime, how many were filled with hope? And when you left, did you leave with more hope than you had when you entered?

> *God whispers to us in our pleasures, speaks in our conscience,*
> *but shouts in our pains; it is his megaphone to rouse a deaf world.*
> C. S. Lewis, *The Problem of Pain*

ROOMS OF HOPE

The Book of Exodus tells us Israel's great Passover story. Moses, under God's direction, was demanding of Pharaoh that he let the Israelites go into the desert to worship. Pharaoh's heart was hardened, and he refused. God told Moses that, as a final demonstration of His might, the firstborn of all the Egyptian people would die along with the firstborn of the cattle and animals. Everyone, from Pharaoh to the poorest farmer, would lose his firstborn.

God's provision for His people's safety involved a sacrifice. Each household was to select a lamb; smaller households could go together, with one lamb meeting the needs of the members of both households. The lamb was to be without blemish, "a male of the first year" (Ex. 12:5). When they killed the lamb, they were to take some of the blood for a special purpose, then eat the rest of the lamb.

The following verses tell us the instructions God gave for the blood of the lamb. As the people obeyed God's instructions, they were expressing their love for God and their faith in His promises.

> *And they shall take some of the blood and put it on the two door-posts and on the lintel of the houses where they eat it. . . . For I will pass through the land of Egypt on that night, and will strike all the firstborn in the land of Egypt, both man and beast; and against all the gods of Egypt I will execute judgment: I am the LORD. Now the blood shall be a sign for you on the houses where you are. And when I see the blood, I will pass over you; and the plague shall not be on you to destroy you when I strike the land of Egypt.* (Ex. 12:7, 12-13)

Think of the Israelite people, huddled in their living rooms, kitchens and bedrooms, in grim anticipation. Think of the little children unaware of exactly what was happening, but aware something was, something that made their parents anxious, even fearful. Some undoubtedly cried. And parents, quick to anger, shushed them impatiently. And they waited, waited to see if the angel of death would pass over their "rooms of hope" as they did their best to trust in God. The story goes on to tell us that the households who did not trust, did not do as God said, and failed to put blood on their doors, were touched by death that night.

We can't read that story in Exodus 12 without seeing Jesus the Savior standing at each of those doors with His arms outstretched, just as they were on the cross. In John 1:29, John the Baptist says about Jesus: "Behold! The Lamb of God who takes away the sin of the world!" And in 1 Corinthians 5:7, the apostle Paul says, "For indeed Christ, our Passover, was sacrificed for us." For the Hebrew people in Egypt, the blood was a sign of forgiveness and marked the entrance to their "rooms." Truly, the angel passed by these protected homes just as he passes by the hearts of those who have accepted Jesus into them.

In translating John 14:2, some Bible versions say "many mansions" or "many homes," while the New International Version uses the word "rooms." "In my Father's house are many rooms; if it were not so, I would have told you. I am going there to prepare a place for you. And if I go and prepare a place for you, I will come back and take you to be with me that you also may be where I am" (John 14:2-3, NIV).

It's wonderful to be invited to a friend's house and be given your own room. Marilyn Dahlberg is a friend like that. Sandy and I were invited to spend a couple days with her and her husband, John, at their desert home. When we walked into our "guest" bedroom, on the nightstand and on the dresser were framed photographs of Sandy and me with John and Marilyn during other happy occasions. Marilyn had gone before us and prepared that room just for us. We've got our own rooms in heaven waiting for us. Can you imagine that—they're prepared just for us! And not because a couple angels were sent ahead to get things ready, but because the God of the universe prepared it for us personally. I can see that room now, with snapshots of us with the Lord on the dresser.

Without a doubt this heavenly room will be continually filled with joy and hope. And it won't just be a room, nor just a suite of rooms, it's going to be a mansion with many rooms. The Bible says that while you're here on earth, you're storing up treasures in heaven. Who knows? You may be decorating your rooms right now, filling them with blessings that are equal to your commitment to God and your love for people.

Isn't it interesting to read the account of Jesus Christ's birth in Bethlehem? When Joseph and Mary arrived, they went to a hotel to find lodging, and the Bible says: "And she brought forth her firstborn son, and wrapped Him in swaddling cloths, and laid Him in a manger; because there was no room for them in the inn" (Luke 2:7). It would appear this was a "room of lost hope" for Joseph and Mary, but God had other plans for the birth of His son.

We have all gone to places where we weren't accepted, or where our welcome was less than we'd hoped it would be. At those times there was "no room in the inn" for us, as well.

SHARING HOPE WITH OTHERS

Sharon Pearce was a full-time registered nurse in a very large hospital in San Diego. She assisted at abortions. After a while, this job started to wear her down. She came to the point where she just couldn't do that kind of work anymore. Finally, the hospital where she worked consented to abort a baby more than seven months along. This pushed Sharon over the edge emotionally. When we spoke I shared a verse from the Book of Proverbs with her. It is the same verse I've stood by in my ministry for over 30 years, a verse that shows me how God looks at those too weak to help or defend themselves.

> *Open your mouth for the speechless,*
> *In the cause of all who are appointed to die.*
> *Open your mouth, judge righteously,*
> *And plead the cause of the poor and needy.*
> (Prov. 31:8-9)

In 1984 Sharon started a ministry called Silent Voices to serve mothers who were in need of help and counsel. Those who came were mostly young women, some teens, mostly poor, asking about abortion and what they should do with their unwanted babies. Through Sharon's ministry, well over 1,000 babies have been born who were destined to die. Since the early beginnings of Silent Voices, Sharon has looked to God to direct her and to provide the services needed to help these distraught women. Silent Voices has offices in Africa, Russia, Israel, Romania, and throughout the United States. Her services now include post-abortion counseling and seminars. Sharon told me recently that the women come for a variety of services, including pregnancy tests, pregnancy/abortion education, questions about sexually transmitted diseases, parenting classes, and post-abortion care. During 2001 Sharon's ministry saved 70 babies in Zambia, Africa, and helped to support the mothers there.

In her own words she relates the joy of having *rooms filled with hope:* "One of the most memorable moments for me was when I witnessed the birth of one of 'our' babies! The mother and I had become quite close during her pregnancy, and she asked me to coach her through labor. I took the Christian-prepared childbirth classes with her [offered at our church, Horizon Christian Center] and was with her when her little boy was born. As I stood and watched this new little life take his first breath, I was overwhelmed with a sense of joy and awe at the miracle that I had witnessed—and the realization that, had Silent Voices not been there when his mother found out that she was pregnant, his life would have been tragically ended through abortion. I'm still moved with emotion as I write this—seventeen years later!"

Over the years when women have come to Sharon and her helpers they have come *without* hope. When they leave Silent Voices they never leave a "room of lost hope." They leave with encouragement, comfort, love and acceptance—and lots of hope.

Karen Johnson is the wife of Pastor Jeff Johnson in Downey ,California. Jeff pastors a church he started with ten people several years ago. He has a congregation of 10,000 members today. Karen had a burden for pregnant young women who were considering an abortion. Her solution has brought hope to thousands, just as Sharon Pearce has. Karen links up the mother of the unborn baby with a family who wants to adopt the child. Karen named her work The House of Ruth.

When people leave the loving atmosphere of The House of Ruth they do not leave a "room of lost hope." Instead both the mother and the future parents find the hope of God in each other.

May I introduce you to a room that can change your life? Perhaps you have visited this room, or do visit it often. Some say they've been wounded in this room or just don't like it. But ultimately, this is the room of all rooms, if managed correctly. It is the House of the Lord, a place where you should be able to go to sit down and find life's answers. It's a place designed by God for hurting people to find hope, comfort, and acceptance. It is known as the church, and this should be a place for you to sit and listen to God's Word and understand the plan He has for you.

While you sit alone in a small, out-of-the-way chapel, or sit surrounded by a crowd in God's house, you're in His presence, and when you're there, His love reigns supreme. When you combine what we spoke about in previous chapters—such as reading your Bible on a regular basis, praying unceasingly, and fellowshipping with God's children, with regular visitation of His house—you will find the healing and closure you're looking for. But you may have had bad experiences "at church," and it is true that not all churches represent the loving God of the Bible. But it is true that He can guide you to the church that you'd feel most comfortable in. Why not simply pray and ask God for the directions to His house right now?

Dear God,

I have come and gone from so many rooms that have taken my hope. Please direct me to Your house. Help me, God, to find Your love and forgiveness. Help me, God, to find peace in the midst of my Ground Zero.

Please, God, open my eyes to see You standing outside of the "rooms of lost hope" that I have frequented in the past.

In Jesus' name I ask for Your help.

Amen.

SECTION III:
RECOVERY

CHAPTER 12
EXPECTANCY

And it shall come to pass in that day
That the Lord will whistle for the fly
That is in the farthest part of the rivers of Egypt,
And for the bee that is in the land of Assyria.
They will come, and all of them will rest
In the desolate valleys and in the clefts of the rocks,
And on all thorns and in all pastures.

Isaiah 7:18-19

Once we determine a disaster or critical incident has occurred, we start the rescue effort immediately. In the past few chapters we've taken a look at how we deal with the disaster itself, the problems we face, and the rescue effort we can engage in to keep our world from crumbling. The next few chapters will deal with the recovery effort.

Just to give you an example to show you what I mean, if your Ground Zero is facing a bankruptcy, immediately *recover* all your cancelled checks, loan documents, contracts and all other paperwork related to your financial situation. And remember to find everything. Often there are receipts or records people have kept that they've forgotten about. These forgotten records may be the precise documents needed to salvage what's left of their material world. Just as "for the want of a nail the battle was lost," sometimes one minuscule detail is enough to help us recover from catastrophe. Your Ground Zero may be something else entirely; nevertheless, in the small details of your situation may rest the foundation upon which you can build salvation or success, in which you find recovery.

All America watched on television, listened to radio, read their newspapers, and generally hung on every word as Mayor Rudolph Giuliani prepared the nation—and particularly those with their hearts and lives invested in the *rescue* effort at *the pile*—for the moment when *rescue* would end and the *recovery* effort would begin. It was that moment when time ran out, when it became humanly impossible for anyone trapped in the rubble to have survived without food or water. From that point on, the methods and hope shifted to that of recovering the victims' remains. This is what we want to spend the next few chapters on. How do you recover when your Ground Zero has happened and there is nothing left to rescue?

As a New York firefighter and I talked, there was nothing unusual during the first hour of conversation. One healthy statement he made started, "I am doing okay." But quickly changed to, "Maybe I'm not, or I wouldn't be talking with you, huh?"

A STRANGE STORY

I can remember at eighteen when I was in army basic training. I was sent to Fort Ord, California, a large training facility carved from the coastal sands of Monterey. Vietnam was happening at the time, and most of the recruits figured they were on their way to that jungle the moment training ended. I was just out of high school and, like everyone in my situation, was going through some deep struggles, struggles caused by questions that needed answers—spiritual questions that my sergeant thought best fielded by the chaplain. So I went, and when the chaplain opened his office door I noticed immediately there was a key difference between the two of us—he was a colonel, and I was a private. He was in the thick of his career and I was in the confused waiting room to manhood. I was looking for the answer to life. There had to be more to it than what I was seeing. I believed in God at the time, though I didn't know Him.

I have no recollection of what the chaplain told me. This was probably because I didn't identify with him or the silver bird on his shoulder. I can, however, tell you exactly what the guys in my training unit said when I got back. The very idea that I went to see the chaplain became the source of a barrage of jokes—capped by the ultimate slam: "Only *wimps* go see a chaplain."

So when this FDNY fireman spoke to me, I knew the potential ribbing he might endure for talking to a chaplain. Sometimes it's the inner strength required to overcome that stigma that generally brings spiritually and emotionally healthy people to ministers, priests, or chaplains in times of crisis. His initial statement told me this firefighter was one of those. The story he told, however,—albeit reluctantly at first—was quite unique. And although he told it just to me, it's important I share it with a much larger audience.

It was still a rescue effort, although time was definitely running out. This firefighter's squad was searching a certain area of the pile—an area of twisted steel girders and small pockets of air. It was conceivable that victims could survive in those pockets, and perhaps just a little farther down some might still be trapped alive. But exhaustion had overtaken the rest of the squad and they'd taken a break for coffee. My new friend, however, although just as tired as the rest, remained, only his will at work. Physically and emotionally drained, he said a prayer for strength and for those he might hope to find, then stared down into the forest of twisted steel girders and remains. So tight was his focus that he suddenly became aware of a small, everyday housefly sitting on a girder in front of him. This fly didn't look much different from the houseflies he'd shooed off his porch during summer, except—and this is a big except—it stared eyeball to eyeball with the fireman, a giant creature clad in his safety gear, fireman's coat and hat. They remained there for a while; each fixed on the other, two of God's creatures that were obviously from totally different worlds, coming together by some cosmic coincidence. As he told me the story, my friend suddenly just shook his head defeatedly, "I must be losing it. I am staring at a fly and it's staring back at me."

Then the fly took wing and flew back flips, in complete circles, then landed in front of the firefighter again. After they stared at each other for a minute or two, the fly darted into the air again, hovered for a moment, then did his back flip routine again. "I mean," the firefighter sputtered to me, "it was just an ordinary fly. No human eyes or anything. I really couldn't believe I was seeing this. But, of course, I was. Then, after flying backwards in these big loops, he dove into a hole the size of a quarter. I never saw him again. But after I sat there stunned for a while, just thinking 'No way!' I started to dig into the pile right where the fly had gone. Gently, piece by piece."

The firefighter went on to say how painstakingly he worked to remove debris until he had a hole big enough to stick his head into. When he did, he saw a shaft of clear space beneath. He yelled to his buddies who were resting and told them he'd found an opening that hadn't been searched as yet. He couldn't go down himself because that would be breaking a longstanding rule—no rescuer climbs into a hole without others being topside to keep him from becoming trapped. So, as my new friend lowered himself into the hole, his partners hurried up, and when they arrived they flipped on their flashlights and illuminated the area he was climbing down into. His climb was worth it. About twenty feet down lay a body buried in the rubble, a New York Fireman clothed in his uniform. This was not only an emotional discovery but also a miraculous discovery. Not many firefighters' bodies had been recovered by that time. Although rescue efforts were still underway, this particular recovery brought hope to the FDNY.

Doesn't it seem bizarre that a fly would try to communicate with a human being? Not to mention "dive bomb" into a small opening in the tangled debris? I assured the man telling me this story that he was not going crazy. Actually he had become the recipient of a divine intervention.

EXPECT SURPRISES

When your world begins to crumble, expect the unexpected. God is willing to help you, and He may do it in ways that step outside the norm. He may use the unlikely to do what He wants done. In the Isaiah 55:8-9, God spoke to the people of Israel saying,

> *"For my thoughts are not your thoughts,*
> *Nor are your ways My ways," says the Lord.*
> *"For as the heavens are higher than the earth,*
> *So are My ways higher than your ways,*
> *And My thoughts than your thoughts."*

The Bible tells us that God loves us and that He wants to give us a fruitful and peaceful life, and it's filled with stories of God's intervention in the affairs of mankind. Unusual events can be God's means of working a miracle in your life. Phil Keaggy wrote a song in the 70s with the lyric line, "Disappointment is His appointment." Let's try our best to look expectantly for God's appointment during our times of disappointment.

Take a moment right now to consider this idea—that your recovery may include extraordinary events to accomplish God's will for you. I can tell you, the family of the fireman whose body was discovered buried in the rubble now has closure over the death of their loved one. That fly was on a mission to get a weary rescue worker to look in an area not yet searched. And maybe, just maybe, God will bring something or someone to you so extraordinary that you wouldn't believe it unless you saw it with your own eyes.

One Old Testament story has always encouraged me to be open to God working in unusual ways. It is about a disobedient prophet named Balaam. (You can find this story in chapters 22-24 of Numbers.) Balak, the king of Moab, heard all that Israel had done to the Amorites and was frightened of them. He offered Balaam rewards if he would curse the children of Israel as they marched across the desert toward Moab.

God intervened and told Balaam not to curse the children of Israel because it was God's plan to bless Israel. Being disobedient, Balaam saddled his donkey and rode off into the early-morning sun. Balak's offer was too good to refuse. If the regular diviner's fee wouldn't motivate Balaam, the King "sent princes, more numerous and more honorable" than the first group. "I will certainly honor you greatly, and I will do whatever you say to me," said the king. We've all observed that greed and avarice can cause people to behave in ways they know they shouldn't. We see that with Balaam. He succumbed to the promise of power, position, and wealth.

The story has its funny side to it. In fact, in my mind's eye I see this story as a cartoon complete with punch line and final truth. Often we look back on our lives and see not only *that* our world has fallen apart, we can also see *why*. September 11th, of course, was an obvious terrorist attack. The Twin Towers' collapse, then, was caused by the volcanic heat from the burning jet fuel when it weakened the structure to the point that it could no longer carry the building's weight. But when an individual's world crashes down, the cause may not be so obvious. We may have brought the problems on ourselves. When the collapse is our fault, it's usually because we've made faulty decisions.

God's anger burned against Balaam because he went with the nobles of Balak. The Angel of the Lord, acting as an adversary against Balaam, stood in the way. The donkey saw the angel, sword drawn, blocking the way, and turned aside and went into a field. Balaam, oblivious to the angel, struck the donkey and ordered him back on the road. Next, the angel blocked a narrow path between two vineyard walls. And when the donkey saw the angel, she pushed herself against one of the walls and crushed Balaam's foot against it; so he hit her again. Then the angel moved farther down the road and stood in a place so narrow the donkey couldn't get by at all. So she lay down in the road! In a great fit of temper Balaam beat her again with his staff.

What a sight! This donkey with all four legs spread out like the points of a compass, her belly in the dirt, her big ears standing straight up like a jackrabbit's, and her eyes bugged out like saucers!

Next comes the most amazing part of the story:

Then the Lord opened the mouth of the donkey, and she said to Balaam, "What have I done to you, that you have struck me these three times?"

And Balaam said to the donkey, "Because you have abused me. I wish there were a sword in my hand, for now I would kill you!"
(Num. 22:28-29)

Imagine that—a man so blinded by his own desires, he carries on a conversation with a donkey! He not only communicates with the animal, he reasons with it and actually answers the donkey's questions.

Now comes the revelation that shows this prideful prophet his world has just collapsed—a collapse he caused because he didn't consider the ramifications of his decision to take matters into his own hands.

Then the Lord opened Balaam's eyes, and he saw the Angel of the Lord standing in the way with His drawn sword in His hand; and he bowed his head and fell flat on his face. (Num. 22:31)

Prior to this moment Balaam's eyes had been blinded, now God opens them. The arrogance of this man melts like butter on a hot skillet in front of this mighty personage from heaven.

And the Angel of the Lord said to him, "Why have you struck your donkey these three times? Behold I have come out to stand against you, because your way is perverse before Me. The donkey saw Me and turned aside from Me these three times. If she had not turned aside from Me, surely I would also have killed you by now, and let her live."

And Balaam said to the Angel of the Lord, "I have sinned, for I did not know You stood in the way against me. Now therefore, if it displeases You, I will turn back." (Num. 22:32-34)

THE ROAD TO RECOVERY

When I've dealt with people and their problems I've found they often didn't know they were heading for destruction. Just like Balaam, people make decisions and head off on their own, sometimes in the wrong direction.

However, when Balaam discovered he'd taken that wrong turn he did something important. He confessed that he'd sinned. The Bible tells us, "all have sinned and fall short of the glory of God" (Rom. 3:23). Balaam did the right thing in confessing his sin. But right afterward, he takes matters back into his own hands, unwilling to go back home and start all over again.

Recovery can take many forms. There are "recovery groups" for every condition under the sun—eating disorders, alcoholism, drug abuse, among others. Not only are there numerous groups, there are numerous recovery programs. Most have been of value to those who commit to them. Others, like Balaam's, are "self-help."

A self-help approach might involve thinking, as Balaam did, that you have to turn on your heels and go all the way back to the beginning to clear up the problem. Or in some cases, decide you have to go through so many "steps" to recover when your world falls apart. Personally, I agree with the next statement make by the Angel to Balaam. He didn't say go back to the beginning. and try to start over. The angel told him, "Go with the men, but only the word that I speak to you, that you shall speak" (Num. 22:35).

This is a picture of heavenly recovery. And it's simple, concise, and clear, just like communication should be. *Go!* That's pretty simple isn't it? In my own life I have found this truth to be a *one-step* program—*go, but go with God!* When your world falls apart, turn to God's way. Of course, it's probably easier to do things your own way, probably your way is the wrong way. Then when we "blow it" we think we have to do something spectacular to get things right. Or we live in denial, self-pity, depression, or some other unnecessary emotional state. Or, thinking that our way will make us right with our neighbor, our God, or ourselves, we gravitate toward a self-help plan.

But instead of turning to self, or some other man-inspired recovery program, we need to turn to the recovery program inspired by God. We need to turn to His tender touch, whether we're trying to recover from the devastating loss of a loved one, a bankruptcy, a job loss, or whatever it may be. And appropriating that wondrous touch for our confused and breaking hearts, we need to rely on these basic facts:

First, God is there, and He cares. The Bible says, "casting all your care upon Him, for He cares for you" (1 Peter 5:7). Go to Him in prayer, speak to Him from your heart as you would a trusted friend,—a friend who can make a huge difference in your life. Give your cares and concerns to Him. Lay them at His feet, not because you're unwilling to face your own problems, but because you know those cares belong with Him and that He has promised to help.

Then, know God loves you and He will help you through these difficult times. As I've mentioned before, the Bible tells us unequivocally, "all things work together for good, to those who love God" (Rom. 8:28). That promise gives us hope for now and for our future—short-term and long-term.

Let me encourage you once again. By keeping your focus on the Lord, by placing your trust solely in Him, by listening to His Word and guiding your steps by it, you will recover from the deep wounds and hurts of life. My pastor, Chuck Smith, has told me for over thirty years, "Time heals all wounds."

If you have never given your heart and life to God, consider doing so today. You see, when God is working in your life, your problems become His problems. Jesus said,

> Come to Me, all you who labor and are heavy laden, and I will give you rest.
> Take My yoke upon you and learn from Me, for I am gentle and lowly in heart, and you will find rest for your souls. (Matt. 11:28-29)

It's not an arduous process to have God take over your life. It's just one simple prayer away. Jesus said, "I am the way, the truth, and the life. No one comes to the Father except through me" (John 14:6). The reason Jesus Christ was crucified on the cross was because of our sins. He died in our place. Now you never need to die. Though your body will die, the real you will live forever and you will be given a new body in heaven. If you confess your sins, God is faithful and just to forgive you of your sins and cleanse you of all unrighteousness. (See 1 John 1:9.) If you are headed in the wrong direction, God will be gracious and merciful to stop you.

If your world is disintegrating financially, emotionally, physically, or spiritually, as it did for Balaam, then listen to this biblical truth to help you. It is time-proven. In 2 Corinthians 5:17 the apostle Paul told the early Christian community, "if anyone is in Christ, he is a new creation; old things have passed away; behold, all things have become new." To me this is the best "recovery program" ever revealed. Become a new creation and let the past go. This takes faith and of course faith is a miracle in itself.

God can use something like the fly communicating with the fireman or a donkey talking to a prophet. Be prepared. Live in an attitude of expectancy. God can—and might—do something extraordinary to get your attention. One of those things may be reading this book. After all, an angel of God may have placed this book into your hands. Who knows the many ways these words could have come to you from God? I do know this: if a fly starts staring at you or a donkey starts to talk with you, listen carefully—because your recovery is right around the corner!

CHAPTER 13
FAITH

For we walk by faith, not by sight.

2 Corinthians 5:7

When a disaster strikes, one of the first emotions experienced is shock. That's true for an individual, a family, a city, a state, or a nation. And shock slaps us with disbelief and confusion. The people of the United States were shocked when the news began running nonstop footage of the terrorist attack on the World Trade Center. Most of the world was shocked when the news broke in their countries. The only people we know of who weren't shocked were the Muslim extremists who perpetrated it, or enjoyed the fact that others did, those who've vowed to destroy the "great Satan," America. Barbara Walters interviewed Saudi Arabians in March, 2002. She asked them if they were happy about the September 11th attack. They replied that not all people, but many Muslims throughout the region were indeed happy about the damage inflicted upon the United States.

WHEN THE SHOCK WEARS OFF

At any Ground Zero, for the people involved, their adrenalin starts pumping right away. But the shock wears off, sometimes quickly—because it has to. It quickly becomes time to launch rescue efforts to save people, to get them out of the zone of devastation. But sometimes, particularly when shock hits an individual, responding instantly and rationally becomes difficult. Disorientation can set in. It can force us to grasp at any straw of understanding and subsequent reasoning that might present itself. Only when our heads begin to cool do we find ourselves able to process and come to grips with the enormity of the situation.

Part of the problem is that initially following a large disaster it's apparent the missing could not possibly last more than a few days without water, food, or other necessities. So everyone within the rescue effort works long hours, racing against the clock hoping to save the injured, those buried alive beneath rubble. When time runs out and the possibility that anyone is still alive fades, the recovery effort begins. Recovery, I believe, is the most difficult process.

This phase of any critical incident requires major adjustments from everyone involved. The authorities and the rescue workers need to adjust their search methods. On a personal level, families and friends of the victims need to adjust to the grim fact that their loved ones are not coming home.

If that first shock of your personal ground zero is beginning to wear off, you have probably come through the worst of your rescue effort. You've faced the reality of your situation and it has stabilized. You've done everything you could do to save your marriage or your finances or your relationship with others. Whatever your particular situation is, we can apply the insights gained from New York City's Ground Zero—insights that, hopefully, will get you on your feet again functioning well.

Two days ago the family celebrated my birthday, and I had the joy of putting two of my grandchildren into a big red wagon and walking them around our neighborhood. It was a kick. We laughed and made funny faces at one another, and I pointed out things like the rising moon, airplanes flying overhead, pretty spring flowers, and the neighbor's dogs.

On our way, we stopped to talk with an eighty-three-year old gentleman at the end of our block, whom I knew to be quite a character. He was certainly quite a gardener. His red and yellow flowers filled the area in front of his house with a beautiful fragrance we all enjoyed. But he hadn't always been a gardener; he also flew fighter planes in World War II, escorting bombers from Great Britain to their targets in Germany. On one mission he'd been shot down, then held as a prisoner of war in a German Luftwaffe camp. Just about a year ago, I saw him walking up and down the street with a "walker" to help him stand. Now he walked with no support at all. I asked him how that could be.

"The key to getting old," he said, "is to keep moving. The minute you slow down or stop it's all over. Just keep moving."

Let's take this older, more experienced gentleman's words and apply them to a broader issue. Recovery from your personal Ground Zero is predicated on your need to "keep moving." The minute you stop moving forward it becomes so much harder to bring closure. We must accept that our world has collapsed, we must assure ourselves everything has been done to rescue all that could be salvaged, and now it's time for recovery. Then closure will come. As Chuck Smith said, "Time heals all wounds."

Let's talk about one of those wounds right now.

AT THE END OF YOUR ROPE

September 11th was on a Tuesday. One week later the rubble looked much like it had a week before, like it hadn't even been touched. Even though thousands of man-hours were spent removing debris, the task looked like it could go on forever. The evening was warm, and the bright lights made me forget it was night. We had just prayed with a group of rescue workers who'd brought some bodies out of the rubble and were sadly watching the ambulance head off towards the morgue. The construction and rescue workers replaced their hard hats and went back work. I remember taking out my cell phone and calling my wife. I asked her to pray for the sad situation we were all in. As we talked, my attention was drawn to the area I'd just left. Three people remained there; they looked like they needed help. As I said good-bye to Sandy and took my first steps towards them, I prayed for the right words.

They were members of the Emergency Medical Services (EMS), and they'd been there for nearly two hours staring at "the pile." This was their post, where they'd been stationed, their area of responsibility, and that responsibility was to carry the recovered remains in rescue baskets on the back of an extended golf cart to the ambulance, a few hundred yards away. Then, whoever didn't drive the ambulance would return to the site and wait. "And wait" is the key word here. It's waiting that caused much of the damage. Too much downtime, while being exposed to too much devastation, takes a real toll on you.

This particular group consisted of one man and two women, all in their early to mid twenties. Over the two hours I noticed this group staring at "the pile" as if dazed. Once in a while they'd look slowly around, as if they were running a survey on the unfolding effort they were in the middle of. But even though their heads moved, their eyes didn't, and their expressions remained the same, stoic and uncommunicative. I was concerned that everything might be finally getting to them, and that they were about to "lose it." Soon after I arrived and introduced myself, though, the women opened up. Like so many others whose emotions had been completely worn through, in less than three minutes one woman was pouring her heart out. She was concerned about the future, fretting over the possibility of further terrorist attacks, and wondering aloud if her children would live to see a happy life. A lot went on behind those glazed eyes. The young man sitting next to her, whose nerves had probably had all their sensitivity beaten out of them, looked up with deadened eyes and said honestly, "I don't want to talk."

When you're recovering from any heart-wrenching experience, it's very easy to have that "deer in the headlights" look. The glazed-over eyes, staring at a fly on the window across the room or the wax fruit on the coffee table, are signs that the brain is trying to process the unprocessible, and that you've grown bone weary trying to do so. The brain, and everything warm surrounding it, is exhausted. If you reach this point of exhaustion, you're working too hard.

Like these EMS workers. They remind us that when we reach total exhaustion, or see that we're on our way to it, we need to pull back from the situation and rest. We need to face the fresh wind for a moment to catch our breath. And there's no finer time, when this fresh air enters our lungs, to let the Holy Spirit enter our lives. He brings guidance and a strong, gentle hand to help bring you out of the past, through the present, and into a promising future. But who is this Holy Spirit? You may not know about Him, because He doesn't blow His own horn very much. But He sure knows you. He is the third Person of the "godhead." The Bible teaches that God revealed Himself to mankind as Father, Son, and Holy Spirit—what's come to be known as the Trinity. The apostle Paul instructed his young student Timothy concerning this subject. Here is what he taught him:

> *And without controversy great is the mystery of godliness:*
> *God was manifest in the flesh,*
> *Justified in the Spirit,*
> *Seen by angels,*
> *Preached among the Gentiles,*
> *Believed on in the world,*
> *Received up into glory.*
> (1 Tim. 3:16)

GOD SHOWS HIMSELF

Simply put, the things of God are a mystery to us. We may never understand it all, but we know He's given us a revelation of Himself through His Son, Jesus. When we learn about Jesus, we learn about God. Jesus' disciples discussed these issues, and the beloved apostle John wrote down the gist of one of those discussions, including what Jesus, Himself, told them:

Thomas said to him, "Lord, we do not know not where you are going, and how can we know the way?"

Jesus said to him, "I am the way, the truth, and the life. No one comes to the Father except through Me. If you had known Me, you would have known My Father also; and from now on you know Him and have seen Him."

Philip said to him, "Lord, show us the Father, and it is sufficient for us.

Jesus said to him, "Have I been with you so long, and yet you have not known Me, Philip? He who has seen Me has seen the Father; so how can you say, 'Show us the Father? Do you not believe that I am in the Father, and the Father in Me? The words that I speak to you I do not speak on My own authority; but the Father who dwells in Me does the works. Believe Me that I am in the Father and the Father in Me, or else believe Me for the sake of the works themselves." (John 14:5-11)

It takes faith to believe the Scriptures, and it takes faith to believe and act upon God's plan. Faith seldom comes easily. It's not something most of us grew up with in our homes. And we're certainly not taught about faith in our public schools. I can't remember having one class on what faith means, or how to live by faith. Faith is a foreign subject to all of us. It is actually part of the mystery Paul was discussing with Timothy. He expressed the following to the church in Rome: "So then faith comes by hearing, and hearing by the word of God" (Rom. 10:17).

This is exactly why it is so crucial for you to pick up a Bible and start reading it. It's filled with God's words. It is God's responsibility to speak to you and help you recover. God often uses people around you—friends, family, neighbors—to help restore you to what is true. But nothing brings a more permanent recovery than God's own word. Contrary to popular opinion, The Bible isn't a stuffy religious book at all. It's filled with stories about people struggling with every aspect of life. And these are all kinds of people— young and old, rich and poor, weak and powerful, king and commoner, and all the stops in between. Many of these people lost loved ones, reputations, hope, and some even lost their lives.

No matter what struggle I'm having, no matter what struggles those I counsel are having, I've always been able to find similar stories in Scripture. And from those examples, I can determine how God would have me act in any particular situation in which I find myself. In all situations we can easily see that God is watching and working, often quietly behind the scenes, on His children's behalf.

Let's look at the apostle Paul's own words as he describes some of the troubles he's encountered in his life as a Christian servant.

From the Jews five times I received forty stripes minus one. Three times I was beaten with rods; once I was stoned; three times I was shipwrecked; a night and a day I have been in the deep; in journeys often, in perils of waters, in perils of robbers, in perils of my own countrymen, in perils of the Gentiles, in perils in the city, in perils in the wilderness, in perils in the sea, in perils among false brethren; in weariness and toil, in sleeplessness often, in hunger and thirst, in fastings often, in cold and nakedness—besides the other things, what comes upon me daily: my deep concern for all the churches. (2 Cor. 11:24-28)

Sounds a little like a gauntlet, doesn't it? Needless to say, Paul had his hands full all the time. Yet through all the Ground Zeros in his life, he ended up triumphant. "Yet in all these things we are more than conquerors through Him who loved us (Rom. 8:37).

I bet there were times when even Paul stared at "the pile" wondering if he would ever experience anything rational again, or even see the sun come up one more time. Paul had to face those make-or-break trials and tribulations of life, just as we do. And as he faced them Paul had to live by faith. His faith was in a God, through the Lord Jesus, who always reached out and saved everyone who was sinking, if they simply called on His name.

Paul continued his life stories to the church at Corinth this way:

In Damascus the governor, under Aretas the king, was guarding the city of the Damascenes with a garrison, desiring to apprehend me; but I was let down in a basket through a window in the wall, and escaped from his hands. (2 Cor. 11:32-33)

LIVING BY FAITH

You might think Paul would end up a "basket case" with all the pressure on him. As it turned out, the opposite was true; he found peace in the midst of those struggles because he always trusted God to help him. He always recovered from his collapsing world; he was always rescued from his Ground Zeros. You may say, "Well of course he did! He was an apostle and had special privileges that common folk like us don't have." Actually he had so much help because he loved, trusted, and had faith in God. It's this faith that will get you up and "moving." Faith like you never had before nor even dreamed of. The only way this faith will grow is if you actively work to grow it. You need to read your Bible daily and let its warm glow of love fill every broken area of your soul.

When King Solomon dedicated the temple in Jerusalem he gave a wonderful prayer to God. Solomon's words are recorded in 1 Kings 8:55-58:

> *Then he stood and blessed all the assembly of Israel with a loud voice, saying: "Blessed be the LORD, who has given rest to His people Israel, according to all that He promised. There has not failed one word of all His good promise, which He promised through His servant Moses. May the LORD our God be with us, as He was with our fathers. May He not leave us nor forsake us, that He may incline our hearts to Himself, to walk in all His ways, and to keep His commandments and His statutes and His judgments, which He commanded our fathers."*
> (1 Kings 8:55-58)

Take note: "There has not failed one word of all His good promise," and this is as true today for you in the midst of your calamity as it was for Solomon and Paul. God will not fail in one word of His good promise to never leave you or forsake you. The Bible says, "Draw near to God and He will draw near to you" (James 4:8).

It wasn't long after I started talking to the female EMS worker that tears began to flow. And soon thereafter, all three wanted to pray and find peace in their lives. Each realized that the long hours and the brutality of this most abnormal of situations had tested their inner strength beyond any normal capacities. They understood they were running on empty and it was this exhaustion that caused them to gaze numbly off into space. Now a life preserver of hope had been thrown into their desperate waters; they grabbed hold and allowed it to pull them to shore. Once this emotional journey had broken the tension, we talked for a while and, believe it or not, we laughed a little too. Finally, our conversation at an end, we shook hands, then hugged each other. And just as we parted, an FDNY commander stepped up. "We need your help; we're bringing out two more bodies."

As I mentioned earlier, the recovery phase of a critical incident can be the most difficult. We're launching ourselves into uncharted waters. Here we are in the midst of a storm, the "eye" is passing overhead and daylight bursts through. We are in a daze and numbed by the experience, and we are not sure if things will ever be the same again. Listen carefully; it's time "to get moving." And at a time like this, you can only move by faith.

CHAPTER 14
STRENGTH

Fear not; for I am with you;
Be not dismayed; for I am your God.
I will strengthen you,
Yes, I will help you,
I will uphold you with My righteous right hand.

Isaiah 41:10

By having give-and-take conversations with so many emergency personnel, within a short time we saw patterns developing, patterns that helped us keep a perspective as we counseled. One very apparent one involved the reaction emergency workers had when they found human remains, particularly hands.

Several times when we spoke to these workers after they'd discovered arms or hands in the rubble, they'd mention wedding rings. This always impacted me. Those rings were the clearest of indicators that a deep human connection had ended, a love had been shattered, and somewhere a husband or wife now faced disconnectedness and profound loneliness. But even though I was impacted, the emergency workers who made the discovery were affected even more.

You see, the wedding rings reminded the search-and-rescue people of their own marriages, their own families. These folks worked ten, twelve, fourteen hours each day—and often seven days a week. Some of the construction workers—those on the cranes, those walking the girders—worked seven days a week for several months after September 11th. The toll on the families of all these hard-working men and women was huge then, and as the years roll on, as relational wounds fester, then hemorrhage, it may become even bigger in the years to come, unless God graciously comes to their aid. It crossed my mind more than once in the days following the Twin Towers collapse, what if New York City were hit with another disaster anywhere near the magnitude of September 11th? How would the city react? The city itself is traumatized, and will be for years, and the emergency services are worn to a frazzle. Please pray for these people and the people of New York City.

HOLDING HANDS

No story has returned to mind over the past year more often than this one. It, too, is about hands, two hands, and it was told to us one night at the morgue. These two hands, nothing else, clasped together, were recovered much like all remains were. The debris hiding them was removed and there they were, two hands clasped tightly, a man's hand holding, and being held by, a woman's hand. From the instant I was told about them, I wondered who those two people were, and how they came to be locked together that way. Were they husband and wife? Boyfriend and girlfriend? Or were they co-workers who sought comfort for one another? Did they decide to face desperation and jump together? Did they join hands inside the building coming down stairs? Were they trapped in one of the upper floors? Were they praying together? We will never know until we get to heaven. What we do know is that these two people found peace in the midst of a storm by taking the hand of the other person. When fear strikes, nothing substitutes for taking the hand of a friend for comfort.

My Uncle George was a bear of a man and, as if to honor his size, he gave me a golden, medium-sized Teddy Bear for Christmas when I was two. The instant he walked in with it, I pointed excitedly and named the animal "Brown Bear." Brown Bear is still with me these many years later. He sits in my home study devotedly watching me as I pray, read my Bible, and prepare my Sunday messages. To look at him you wouldn't be too impressed. His fur is mostly worn away, he has one eye missing, he's missing some stuffing (which makes his shape a little irregular), one ear has been chewed on, and his nose and mouth have lost much of their definition. Although most might think he's definitely showing his age, I see something entirely different. I see a friend who's been with me my whole life, and was particularly faithful in my younger years. When I was little and got frightened, maybe by a raging storm scratching at my window, it was Brown Bear I hugged and rubbed, and who eventually gave up his fur for me. When I was a little older, when I realized I had problems, it was Brown Bear who was always there to listen to them and console me when the lights were out. I've kept Brown Bear as the only possession linking me to my childhood. When I was a young father, Brown Bear was always there to remind me that I should be gentle with my children, and when they were frightened that I should always be there for them. Brown Bear is my "clasped hands" in a disintegrating world. He reminds me how fragile life is, and that I should never lose the wide-eyed innocence of childhood.

STRENGTH

When the Beatles burst on the world music scene in the early '60s, one of their first hits was *I Want to Hold Your Hand*. This tune topped the record charts in both the United Kingdom and the United States, and from December 1963 through January 1964 it was the number-one record in the world. It actually stayed in the top fifty for more than twenty-two weeks— the song obviously striking a chord with people around the globe. But why?

One reason might be that our hands are extensions of ourselves. When we hold somebody's hand, we extend our life to theirs; even *join* our lives. And after we've walked hand-in-hand like that for a while—maybe along a country road when fall is ablaze, or along a sandy beach at a crimson sunset—even though only our hands are touching, we feel connected in so many different ways. It's as if each finger joins a thousand threads between us, tying heart to heart, vision to vision, breath to breath. Saying "I want to hold your hand" is saying "I want to be connected"— a part of another person. All of us want that.

OTHER HANDS

To dig a little deeper, let's take a look at more ways the English language uses the word *hand*: lend a hand, give someone a hand, I hand it to you, get a hand on it, hands free, handoff, hands off, handbook, handbill, handbrake, handbag, handful, handhold—on and on the words and phrases flow. The weight-lifter version of a dictionary I have has even more uses, more than a hundred, actually.

Recently two of my police officer friends had to shoot suspects they encountered on patrol. Both incidents involved hands. They occurred weeks apart, but both were painful for my friends, and it took both friends quite a while to regain the peace they had had before. In one case the suspect resisted arrest when he broke lose from a second police officer's grip, then ominously reached beneath the seat of his car. While down there for a split second, he seemed to grab something. Springing back up, he spun toward the second officer. Fearing for his partner's life, my friend fired.

In the second incident, a guy got into a hand-to-hand battle with the arresting officer. Thrown back, the guy picked up a large rock and charged the officer with it. Standing between the guy and bystanders, the officer knew that if he didn't stop him, the guy would kill him and probably go on to kill a bystander or two. So my friend shot him. Critical incidents like those are true disasters, complete with a rescue effort, a recovery process, and—finally—

closure. But they also have something else in common. In both cases, something that could cause harm, even death, was in the hands of an assailant.

This story, found in the Book of Genesis, tells of history's first murder, which occurred in history's first family. Cain and Abel were the sons of Adam and Eve. "Now Cain talked with Abel his brother; and it came to pass, when they were in the field, that Cain rose against Abel his brother and killed him" (Gen. 4:8).

We don't know what these brothers talked about, nor do we know why their conversation led to murder. We can tell from the original language that it was heated, at least from one side of it. The word translated "against" describes motion towards something or someone. And in this text, it undoubtedly retains some of the original sense of physical and mental motion, or emotion, one towards the other. It shows us that when people use their hands for good or bad, it takes both a physical and mental resolve.

Have you ever heard of a metonymy? An example of a metonymy is "hitting the bottle," which describes a heavy drinker. A metonymy is a figure of speech that consists of the use of the name of one object or concept for that of another to which it is related. The Old Testament gives us an example of a hand metonymy in 1 Samuel 22:17: "Then the king said to the guards who stood about him, "Turn and kill the priests of the Lord; because their hand also is with David, and because they knew when he fled and did not tell it to me." Saul was saying the priests helped David with their counsel and with food and didn't betray him. All this is contained in, and expressed by, the word "hand."

Last night Renae, my secretary, *gave her hand* in marriage to Gordon, now her new husband, and I performed the ceremony. When the time came for the exchange of rings, I recited, "Please join right hands and face each other." They did, then repeated the words I spoke: "With this ring I thee wed, in the name of the Father, and of the Son, and of the Holy Ghost." As each slipped the ring on their beloved's ring finger, they clasped their loved one's opposite hand. In a real sense, their connection to one another was complete.

JESUS' HANDS

It's critical that you, too, have a hand to hold during your time of upheaval and hurt. And there's no better hand to grab than the Lord's. After all, He's put this book into your *hands* to bring you hope. Use Him as your "Brown Bear," hold Him close to your heart, and let the Lord's comfort wash away your fear and strengthen you. On resurrection morning, among the first words Jesus said after He emerged from the tomb were "rejoice" and "don't be afraid." Isn't that amazing? Jesus had just triumphed over what for us would have been an eternity in hell, and He's telling the women who came to His tomb, "Be glad and don't be afraid." The women, had they looked at the wounds in His hands, would have completely understood His message. It's because of these nail-pierced hands that we can all rejoice. And rejoicing chases away fear; there is nothing for us to fear anymore. Jesus has conquered death for all who will simply believe.

The prophet Zechariah recorded a verse that points to the returning Messiah. "And someone will say to him, 'What are these wounds in your hands?' Then he will answer, 'Those with which I was wounded in the house of my friends'" (Zech. 13:6).

The writer of Hebrews says, "But we see Jesus, who was made a little lower than the angels, for the suffering of death crowned with glory and honor, that He, by the grace of God, should taste death for everyone" (Heb 2:9. He goes on to say, ". . . and release those who through fear of death were all their lifetime subject to bondage" (Heb. 2:15).

What wonderful promises these two Scriptures are for you and me. We, like all of mankind, have experienced that sometimes not-so-subtle gnawing at our souls that tells us someday we're going to die. It's such an uncomfortable feeling to know that one day we'll wake up, and it will be our last day. The Bible tells us clearly it's this fear of death that keeps us in bondage. But Jesus has now emerged from the tomb to say, "Be glad; don't be afraid."

Jesus' hands were nailed to the cross when the Romans crucified Him. And those nail-scarred hands are going to be the subject of intense discussion in the future. I can't help but think those nails are beautiful. In a way, they're like wedding rings. Scripture identifies the church as the bride of Christ, and in the Book of Revelation, when speaking of the church, Scripture says the bride has prepared herself and made herself ready. Just as Renae proclaimed her love for Gordon by presenting him with a ring, Jesus showed us the depth of His love for us by taking those nails into His hands and dying for us.

In God's Hands

Often people forget God is a big God, yet for all of His power and infinite glory, He is able to express Himself so that we're able to understand.

Here's an amazing Scripture about the mighty hand of God:

Who has measured the waters in the hollow of his hand,
Measured heaven with a span
And calculated the dust of the earth in a measure?
Weighed the mountains in scales
And the hills in a balance?
(Isa. 40:12)

How utterly fantastic to read these few words and understand the awesome power and infinite size of God? Isaiah tells us God, who created the Earth, is so much larger than the Earth. Remember, Earth's diameter is 7,090 miles, yet it's only one minor planet in the entire universe. We can't measure its waters in the hollow of our hand, and the universe in its span—but God does so easily. A *span* is the distance between the end of the expanded thumb and little finger. How big is the universe? I don't know for sure, but what I do know is that light takes over 100,000 years to travel from one side of the Milky Way, our galaxy, to the other—and light travels at 186,000 miles per second. And as big as that is (I'll let you do the math), our Milky Way is only one of billions of galaxies in our universe. And all that fits in the span of God's hand.

Like Isaiah, King David was captivated by God's magnificence as well. In Psalm 8 he declares:

When I consider Your heavens,
the work of Your fingers,
The moon and the stars,
which You have ordained,
What is man that You are mindful of him,
And the son of man that You visit him?
(Ps. 8:3-4)

King David is absolutely right. What are we that God would want to involve Himself in our little lives when His creation is so enormous and we are so trifling? "He counts the number of the stars; He calls them all by name" (Ps. 147:4).

No great astronomer from Cal Tech or MIT, or any other great university, can tell us how many stars there are. In fact, it takes huge computers to track just the stars we do know about, and catalog their names and locations. God counts these and trillions more, and calls all of them by name. I am not sure I could even tell you where my car keys are right now, let alone name just fifty stars.

Here's another example to help you put God's might into perspective and how He is the ultimate "helping hand." In the constellation Orion the hunter's left shoulder is a red, "twinkling" star named Betelgeuse. Actually Betelgeuse doesn't "twinkle"—it pulsates. This pulsation occurs when its gases expand and contract, beating much like your heart. When it expands to its fullest size, Betelgeuse is 400 million miles in diameter; when it contracts, it's only 270 million miles in diameter. This one star is so huge that when contracted, if you had a big enough cookie cutter, you could punch a circle in the star's center 100 million miles in diameter, place our sun in the hole, let our earth orbit it at 93 million miles away, and you'd still have more than 100 million miles to jog to reach the star's exterior. Although it's a big star, Betelgeuse is not the largest star out there. That is exactly what Paul the Apostle told the Corinthians 2,000 years ago. "There is one glory of the sun, and another glory of the moon, and another glory of the stars; for one star differs from another star in glory" (1 Cor. 15:41).

And to think, God just places those stars out there with his fingertips. Can't you see how you can use His help today? He wants to take you by the hand and walk with you through this splintering world of yours. And He also wants to help rebuild it. God is not some huge religious fanatic perched on a throne somewhere that you can't reach. He is near. The Bible says, "Draw near to God and He will draw near to you" (James 4:8). Let Him give you a hand and walk with you.

One night at dinner with several NYPD police officers, their commanding officer told me an amazing tale. A few short days after the towers crumbled, a team of professional athletes rode a ferry from New Jersey to the pier near Ground Zero. Not wanting to leave the ferry's safety, they sent their public relations guy to Ground Zero to grab someone in charge. "Find someone appropriate," the public relations guy said. The team wanted to shake hands with the police officers working the site. One policeman told me, "Here were these million-dollar bodies wanting to shake our hands. We told them we didn't need anyone to shake our hands—we needed people to lend a hand." God isn't looking for a photo opportunity with you, He wants to take your hand and lend His strength to it. He wants to give you a hand—the hand of all hands.

Read with me the Twenty-third Psalm. Picture the person the psalmist describes, the one in adversity, the one who's put his trust in God and whom God is leading. If you do the same today, God will help you recover.

> *The LORD is my shepherd;*
> *I shall not want.*
> *He makes me to lie down in green pastures;*
> *He leads me beside the still waters.*
> *He restores my soul;*
> *He leads me in the paths of righteousness*
> *For His name's sake.*
> *Yea, though I walk through the valley of the shadow of death,*
> *I will fear no evil;*
> *For You are with me;*
> *Your rod and Your staff, they comfort me.*
> *You prepare a table before me in the presence of my enemies;*
> *You anoint my head with oil;*
> *My cup runs over.*
> *Surely goodness and mercy shall follow me*
> *All the days of my life;*
> *And I will dwell in the house of the LORD*
> *Forever.*
> (Ps. 23:1-6)

> *Thus says the Lord of hosts:*
> *"Let your hands be strong,*
> *You who have been hearing in these days*
> *These words by the mouth of the prophets . . ."*
> (Zech. 8:9)

When God holds your hand, you will have all the strength you need.

CHAPTER 15
PERSEVERANCE

*And let us not grow weary while doing good, for in due season we
shall reap if we do not lose heart.*

Galatians 6:9

Remember the movie *Moonstruck*.? It starred Cher and Nicolas Cage, and
at least part of it was filmed in the heart of New York's Little Italy at Luna's
Restaurant on Mulberry Street. Whenever I'm in New York I try to eat there at
least once. The décor's nothing to write home about, but the double portion of
spaghetti and meatballs certainly is. And the place has a family feel about it
and real Old World charm, a neat combination when away from home. One
evening a few of us took a break from "the pile" and went to dinner there.

NATURAL QUESTIONS,
NORMAL FEELINGS

In the booth next to us sat a couple police recruits. They'd been on foot
patrol in the neighborhood, and, like us, wanted the taste of a home-cooked
meal. These recruits, a man and a woman, served at least two purposes. By
walking the streets themselves, they freed up some sorely needed full-time
officers for work at the World Trade Center, and at the same time, they
showed a strong presence on the streets, which should help change the minds
of any bad guys hoping to take advantage of this sudden upheaval. I was
struck by how young they looked, not much older than teenagers, to me. I
glanced over at them now and again as I wondered how their Police
Academy studies were going, and how the terrorist attack might have affected them. When dessert came, I managed to strike up a conversation with
them. When they found out I was a police chaplain the ice was broken and
they spoke freely. And they had a lot they wanted to talk about—the attack,
the work at "the pile," the potential for future attacks. And I wanted to know
if the attack had dulled their desire to go into law enforcement. Had they
been frightened enough to quit, or consider quitting? They didn't hold anything back. Both were concerned that if they did continue, if they did eventually became sworn officers, their lives might be lost like the officers at the

Twin Towers. "Maybe we ought to quit now," one of them said.

"And if we don't quit now, I'm not sure I'd last much longer, anyhow," the other added.

"You're not alone in how you feel," I told them. "A number of the veteran officers at 'the pile' I've met over the last ten days, have been asking themselves the same thing. Do I want to take the chance that I'll have to go through this again? Do I want to put my families through this again? Those are big questions." But then I went on to tell them that those same officers had answered their own questions. Most decided that they'd been called to stay faithful to the people they serve, even in horrific times like these. In fact, it's to these very times they have been called, and if they're called again, so be it. What I said to them seemed to help, but what really helped them was to know that those officers senior to them, officers they admired and were gearing up to emulate, had gone through the same questioning they just had. And had decided to stay the course.

Remember this statement from several chapters ago? *The thoughts you are having are normal thoughts that any normal person would have in an abnormal situation.* See how the statement applies to this situation?

The desserts remained untouched as we talked and a warm bond formed between us. These "kids" seemed to be taking to heart my words of encouragement. Why didn't I just let them consider leaving the force? After all, the job's difficult, the pay's okay but not great, and the risk is high and getting higher. Well, just the night before, I'd stepped up to a knot of four or five officers who stood out in front of their temporary headquarters, a motor home beside the morgue. They were bantering back and forth about their retirements, and over the next few months, each planned to kiss full-time duty good-bye. One guy in his fifties had only thirty days left. "And I'm out of here. Let somebody else get blown up by terrorists. In less than a month all you're gonna see of me are my taillights."

"Oh, no, you're not!" came a challenging voice. Next to the motor home was the mobile Salvation Army Canteen, a vehicle with sides that opened up so those inside could serve food. About a dozen officers stood there with sandwiches and drinks. One detective, sipping a hot coffee, had overheard and stepped from the canteen to listen. Now he made his provocative pronouncement.

"Oh, no, you're not what?" The officer with thirty days left fired back.

"You're not going to retire," the detective said, almost coldly. "They've frozen all retirements because of the—well, the present situation here."

"No way!" Officer thirty-days bellowed. "They didn't do that! They can't do that!"

"Sure they did," the detective told him again. As it turned out, he was a union representative who'd been in the meetings in which this word had come down from the mount. Needless to say, the next thirty minutes of conversation were lively and heated. But the detective was right; retirements had been frozen.

About seven months later I spoke with a union representation about NYPD recruitment. He told me that prior to 9/11 about 3,000 recruits went to the six-month NYPD academy yearly. Recruiting that many had become difficult in recent years—so much so, that in one recent year the city spent about $10 million advertising law-enforcement jobs. They'd even had to lower the entrance standards—unfortunately a trend in many large American cities.

In the year 2001 over 3,000 officers retired or left because of injuries and other causes. In 2002 the department expects to lose even more. In twenty-four months, close to 15% of the department will be gone and the number of new recruits won't make up for it. The population of full-time, committed law enforcement officers is on the decline in one of the world's largest cities. That's why I did my best to encourage these young recruits not to give up, to continue with their dream and aspiration of becoming a New York City police officer.

It's normal to seriously think about giving up when our world starts falling apart around us. It often seems we'll never recover nor will we ever experience closure to our hurt and pain. Just to give up, to quit, to throw up one's hands and give all the mess, the turmoil, all the pain to come, to someone else, seems like an attractive idea. When life becomes too hard for us to handle, we want to resign. I've often found this attitude when counseling suicidal people. Life is so overwhelming that the values and ideals they held earlier—such as duty, self-sacrifice, perseverance—no longer seem relevant. They can no longer identify with what they used to think was "normal."

These recruits are no different than you or me. Sometimes life seems just too big to handle. It's like we've suddenly grabbed the end of a fully charged fire hose and it's whipping us around all over the place. We want to let go. We want to resign. In counseling the suicidal we often find this to be their perspective. Life has become just too overwhelming and getting back to the norm seems impossible.

BADGES

Police officers' identities go everywhere with them. This past Easter, two members of the NYPD joined us in San Diego for our Easter Outreach Services. They told those there about their involvement in 9/11, then thanked San Diego for all our city had done to help New York. More than 10,000 people came to hear their firsthand accounts of Ground Zero. Before they left on Sunday afternoon to fly back home they joined my family for Easter dinner. Our three-year-old grandson, Parker, stood in awe of their crisp blue uniforms and shiny badges. They also had a row of colorful decorations honoring elements of their service pinned to their jackets. Parker really liked those.

"Hello, Mr. Policeman," he'd say with great respect. Respect, though, didn't keep him from getting confused. At one point he called the sergeant, "Mr. Police Station." Respect also didn't keep him from getting comfortable with them. After about four hours with them, when they walked to their car, Parker decided it was time to be on a first-name basis with this giant in the blue uniform. He waved to the sergeant, saying, "Good-bye Station."

Yes, the uniforms do identify police officers. Yet Parker called the sergeant "police station" even after he'd gotten out of his uniform and donned street clothes. He knew they were his heroes, in or out of blue. The leather belt, handgun, cuffs, flashlight, and other paraphernalia are also part of an officer's identity. Yet one item identifies a police officer more than any other—the badge. The badge calls out their authority to everyone nearby. And it has different effects on those who hear it. For the bad guys, it (hopefully) strikes fear and brings submission. To the good folks, it means honor, integrity, courage, and servanthood. The New York Port Authority and the New York Police Department have generally the same badge policy. The badges of a patrol officer or a regular police officer are called *white badges*. Detectives, lieutenants, captains, and chiefs all have *gold shields*. Each badge identifies the rank of the officer wearing it, and police officers have a number on theirs. This number identities them to both public and the department.

The landfill on Staten Island was reopened after 9/11. These 175 acres are fourteen miles from Manhattan and it was there New York City brought the over a million tons of debris from the World Trade Center during the first four months. After the debris was brought by barge and truck, 300 police officers combed it systematically for evidence and human remains. In an interview with the Associated Press, Chief of Detectives William Allee said,

"This is not a garbage dump; it's a special place. It is sacred ground to all of us. We're doing God's work and I feel honored to be here."

Several who worked there told me the task was unpleasant at best. The debris is more than just twisted metal, over to the side are stacked more than a thousand automobiles—a vast junkyard stacked two and three high. These cars, taxicabs, police cars, even ambulances, were retrieved from the streets around the twin towers. Also retrieved and placed in another line are about ninety battered fire engines and ladder trucks. Many of them have had their nameplates removed, probably to be displayed at the stations where the trucks once worked. Those nameplates are like badges, badges of honor, an identity for the firefighters. I've heard that one nameplate from a station that lost seven men was bolted onto their new truck in honor of those firefighters.

One policeman told me that while on duty at Staten Island, he found a badge in the rubble. It was twisted and melted, and it was a *white badge*, with the number still discernible. It was identified as belonging to a member of the Port Authority Police. From that moment on, this badge took on a life of its own, and so far it has honored both its owner and all those who fell with him.

My wife, Sandy, spoke to 300 women at a luncheon honoring the wives, moms, and daughters of NYPD officers. While there, she had the honor of meeting seventy-seven-year-old Arlene Howard. Mrs. Howard has two sons, Patrick and George. Patrick is a New York City Police Officer. His brother, George, *was* a New York Port Authority Police Officer. George was forty-four years old, and September 11th was his day off. Yet when he heard about the attack he headed to the scene to do what he could. And if courage could do anything, George would probably do quite a lot. You see, George had been awarded the Medal of Valor in 1993 for helping out during the first World Trade Center bombing; at that time he had sixteen years on the job. During that ordeal, an elevator packed with children was jammed in the shaft. George Howard rescued them all. That had been his day off too. His mother, Arlene, was given his shiny silver badge, the one found at the landfill. She, in turn, give it to President George W. Bush. Mr. Bush held this badge up when he addressed Congress, saying, "I will carry this." Badge 1012 belonged to a hero who loved his job, and that badge became the identity of a true-life hero, a hero who left a wife and two sons (thirteen and seventeen years old) behind. He charged into harm's way to help people survive their collapsing world.

OUR ID BADGE

If someone asked you who you are, what your identity is, how would you answer? What do you identify with? *With whom* do you identify? You may discover that you have an identity crisis.

Jesus wants to be your badge of identification; He gave His life for you so that you could identify with Him in His death, burial, and resurrection. Colossians 1:7 says, "Christ in you, the hope of glory." This is an amazing discovery for us, human beings, to make: that God can put His Spirit within us and we can live a new life directed by His power. This is exactly what you've hoped for; this may be what you've been praying for—and didn't know it. True recovery from a disintegrating world means being rescued by Jesus and taking His identity. It is His identity that extricates you from your problems and this collapsing world in which we all live.

What do I mean about Jesus being our identity?

Jesus said, "Unless one is born again, he cannot see the kingdom of God" (John 3:3). You may simply want all the turmoil of your Ground Zero to just "go away," but it is rebirth you seek and may not even know it. The Bible tells us that when Jesus died on the cross, He took your sins upon Himself and became sin for you. Why did He do this? So that you could live for God. If, by faith, you accept what Jesus did for you, and ask Him into your heart and life, then you'll not only be forgiven your sins and trespasses, you will be given eternal life.

Remember I told you I needed a special identification tag hanging around my neck to get into Ground Zero, the morgue, and the Family Assistance Center? If I didn't have this photo ID with all of the special security codes on it, the security people would have turned me away. It was the identification that gave me the access. The Bible tells us that all those who've ever lived have their lives recorded in heaven. But not only recorded, we'll have to give an accounting of our lives when they're done. And we won't be giving this account to our best buddies or our parents; we'll be giving it to God himself. The following verses describe this.

> *Then I saw a great white throne and Him who sat on it, from whose face the earth and the heaven fled away. And there was found no place for them. And I saw the dead, small and great, standing before God, and books were opened. And another book was opened, which is the Book of Life. And the dead were judged according to their*

works, by the things which were written in the books. The sea gave up the dead who were in it, and Death and Hades delivered up the dead who were in them. And they were judged, each one according to his works. Then Death and Hades were cast into the lake of fire. This is the second death. And anyone not found written in the Book of Life was cast into the lake of fire. (Rev. 20:11-15)

Notice these verses tell us that everyone will be accountable to God, no matter what their status on earth. Also note that there are books which have everyone's life written in them, and each person is judged according to what's written there. The fact that there are "books" (plural) tells us that nothing is missed and we're held accountable for every action and every thought. In the second chapter of Romans, the apostle Paul teaches that people's conscience will either excuse or accuse them. The conscience is like a recording machine that captures everything, then accountability occurs according to the good news of Jesus: "In the day when God will judge the secrets of men by Jesus Christ, according to my gospel" (Rom. 2:16).

If there is anything missing in today's society, it's accountability. This accounts for the large problem with pornography in the western world—no accountability to anyone. The lack of accountability has caused the extremely high rates of alcoholism and drug addiction. Accountability must start in the home, where parents show their accountability to one another and the children are taught the consequences of their own actions. If there is no clear authority structure and communication is lacking, then the children grow up without understanding accountability. It's a do-or-die world out there, and if we toss our lives to the wind we reap the whirlwind.

When the books open in heaven, there's another book that'll open alongside it. It's the *Book of Life.* God looks in this book to see what names are found there. If a person's name isn't found, that person is separated from God for eternity. This is the "Who's Who" of heaven. Since this book is so important, we want our name to be found in it. How then do we get our name in there? In the following verse from Revelation we're given a great clue to this mystery. "But there shall by no means enter it anything that defiles, or causes an abomination or a lie, but only those who are written in the Lamb's Book of Life" (Rev. 21:27).

Check out the name of the book. Only those whose names are written in this book are allowed into heaven. It is called the Lamb's Book of Life. If we can identify the Lamb, then we want to identify *with* the Lamb, so He'll put our names into His book.

When John the Baptist baptized people in the wilderness, Scripture says when he saw Jesus walking towards him he said to the people, "Behold! The Lamb of God who takes away the sin of the world!" (John 1:29).

Again, the next day, John stood with two of his disciples. And looking at Jesus as He walked, he said, "Behold the Lamb of God!" The two disciples heard him speak, and they followed Jesus.
(John 1:35-37)

Now we know Jesus is the *Lamb of God* and this *Book of Life* is *His* book. He puts the names of everyone who identifies with Him into that book. When the book is opened and the roll call takes place, will your name be there? If you want it to be, you should do what John's disciples did—you should follow Jesus.

When the Jews came back to Israel after seventy years of Babylonian captivity, they found that Nehemiah had restored Jerusalem's walls and hung her gates. When they arrived, he gathered the people and told them a census would be taken and a registration by genealogy would show who would be allowed to move into the capital.

Now the city was large and spacious, but the people in it were few, and the houses were not rebuilt. Then my God put it into my heart to gather the nobles, the rulers, and the people, that they might be registered by genealogy. And I found a register of the genealogy of those who had come up in the first return, and found written in it: These are the people of the province who came back from the captivity, of those who had been carried away, whom Nebuchadnezzar the king of Babylon had carried away, and who returned to Jerusalem and Judah, everyone to his city. (Neh. 7:4-6)

In the following verses, we see there was a group with an obvious identity crisis. "And these were the ones who came up from Tel Melah, Tel Harsha, Cherub, Addon, and Immer, but they could not identify their father's house nor their lineage, whether they were of Israel" (Neh. 7:61).

In New York City, the government is doing everything humanly possible to identify the remains of those lost on that terrible day. They're using all the latest technology around the clock to complete this monumental task.

How about you? Are you willing to take the eternal identity that God has for you? And it will only take you a few moments. All you have to do is reach out and take His hand and let His Son write your name in His Book of Life. He totally identifies with you, because "God so loved the world that He gave His only begotten Son" (John 3:16). He identifies with your heartache, your loneliness, your questions, and your life.

If your identity is in Him, He will enable you to persevere. Because you can keep going through any difficulty if you know the ending will be worth it all.

> Dear God,
> I do want to identify with You today. I do want You to identify me as one of Your children.
> God, please help me recover my situation. Please fill me with Your love, Your peace and Your hope.
> Dear God, I pray that You would put my name in the Lamb's Book of Life.
> In Jesus name I ask these things,
> Amen.

SECTION IV: CLOSURE

CHAPTER 16
WORD POWER

The Lord gave the word;
Great was the company of those who proclaimed it.

Psalm 68:11

If you've been suffering for some time, you may find it difficult to believe that what you're going through will ever end, that you'll ever bring *closure* to your personal Ground Zero. Closure is the final phase of a critical incident and you need to be assured closure will come and peace will follow.

Have you ever said something and immediately wished you hadn't? Wished you'd let whatever it was pass. Or made what you thought was a clever quip, only to realize it was not all that clever and it may actually have hurt someone? We've all done that—unfortunately, probably many times.

Words can be a powerful force. Benjamin Franklin is credited with coining the phrase "Give me twenty-six lead soldiers and I will conquer the world." Those twenty-six lead soldiers were the twenty-six letters of the alphabet (when typeset). Later Karl Marx, author of *The Communist Manifesto,* would use this same phrase to give birth to a revolution. Both these historical figures knew the value of words, and their lives show us they were very skilled in their use of words.

The collapse of the World Trade Center left behind many memorable words, and makes us look at some words differently. Construction on the World Trade Center began with groundbreaking in 1966, and occupancy began in 1973. Minoru Yamasaki, chief architect of the project, had this to say about his creation: "The World Trade Center is a living symbol of man's dedication to world peace." What a sad statement to read in light of the WTC's destruction and ultimate collapse on September 11, 2001. Read on for more of the chief architect's thoughts on this building.

I feel this way about it. World trade means world peace and consequently the World Trade Center buildings in New York . . . had a bigger purpose than just to provide room for tenants. The World Trade Center is a living symbol of man's dedication to world peace . . .

beyond the compelling need to make this a monument to world peace, the World Trade Center should, because of its importance, become a representation of man's belief in humanity, his need for individual dignity, his beliefs in the cooperation of men, and through cooperation, his ability to find greatness.

In light of 9/11, it seems man's "ability to find greatness" has vanished in the rubble. What Yamasaki meant as a structure to draw people together has become a symbol that draws people to battle.

LAST WORDS

We'll never know all of the last words spoken between loved ones, friends, and victims on September 11th. Was there a wife who had an argument with her husband as he went out the door to work? Did a teenage daughter say something mean and thoughtless to her mother as she left for school and her mom left for Tower One? More than likely, some "last words" were cruel, while others were loving and kind. Whatever those words were, they will impact the survivors for years.

I was also a chaplain during the Oklahoma City bombing. I remember counseling a Federal Agent there who told me he'd been on the phone with one of his best friends in the DEA. These men had known each other for years, and had actually worked cases together. Although they now worked in different buildings and for different law enforcement agencies, they kept in frequent contact. They'd made arrangements to meet for lunch that afternoon. Five minutes after they hung up the phone with each other, the bomb in the Ryder truck out front exploded. This man's friend was killed. He just could not get over the fact that less than five minutes earlier, they'd had their last words with each other.

On Super Bowl Sunday I received a telephone call from a family asking me to go to the hospital and pray for a loved one. His last words had been, "I'll be back in ten minutes." At half-time the young man wanted to go get some more chips and dip. He hopped on his motorcycle, said those last few words to his wife and friends, then roared off. Ten minutes later, the people at the party heard sirens not too far from the house. One person at the party walked down the block and around the corner, and saw his friend being loaded into an ambulance. Someone had run a stop sign and plowed into him. He died from his injuries. His last words—"I'll be back in ten minutes"—still linger in the minds of his friends and family.

TODD BEAMER

Todd Beamer, a graduate of Wheaton College in Illinois, a resident of Hightstown (NJ), an executive with Oracle, husband of Lisa and father of two children and a baby soon to be born, is best remembered by Americans as the man whose last recorded words were, "Let's roll." Todd was aboard United Airlines Flight 93, which crashed in rural Pennsylvania on September 11th, 2001. Though "let's roll" has been coined as Todd's heroic statement, I find it interesting to read the reports of Lisa D. Robinson's conversation with Todd. Lisa was the GTE operator who received Todd Beamer's emergency telephone call from the highjacked plane. Near the end of their time on the phone, Todd recited Psalm 23 with Lisa. ("Yea, though I walk through the valley of the shadow of death, I shall fear no evil: for thou art with me"). Then Todd left the phone off the hook, apparently so she could listen to what unfolded. During the conversation, Todd had asked Lisa to call his wife and tell her he loved her and the kids. When the operator called she told Todd's wife that the last words of Todd Beamer were: "God help me. Jesus help me. Are you ready? Let's roll." I am so thankful—as I am sure Lisa Beamer and all of Todd's friends and family are—to know that the full statement of Todd's last recorded words included this devout Christian man asking for God's help.

Have you ever wondered what your last words will be? And, after you've uttered them, what will their impact be on the people who love you the most? Lisa Beamer, Todd's widow, told the Associated Press, "Some people live their whole lives, long lives, without having left anything behind. My sons will be told their whole lives that their father was a hero, that he saved lives. It's a great legacy for a father to leave his children."

Two other men, Thomas Burnett and Jeremy Glick, joined Todd in the formulation of a plan to overpower the terrorists and take back the plane, even though one of the terrorists in the main cabin was reported to have a bomb strapped to his midsection. Thomas Burnett called his wife from the plane four times on his cell phone. One of those times he said, "I know we're all going to die—there's three of us who are going to do something about it."

Jeremy Glick called his family and told them, "We can take them, we can take them." Glick was six foot two and 220 pounds, of athletic build. His father-in-law, Richard Makely, said he took the phone from his wife who said Jeremy had put the phone down and would be back. He hoped Jeremy would come back on line to tell him the terrorists had been subdued and the pilots were once again in control. Instead he said, "I heard the end of the story."

The pilot, it's been reported from those who've heard the voices from the cockpit recorder, heard these words: "Get out of here! Get out of here!"

LISA BEAMER

As I mentioned earlier, I had the privilege to sit beside Lisa Beamer on stage at the PNC Bank Arts Center amphitheater in Holmdel, New Jersey. I've met a lot of people in my life, but Lisa impressed me far more than most. She is poised, confident, charming, gentle, and radiates God's love. When she was told on Friday her husband's last words, she responded, "It offered some emotional closure and began a new era of hope. It's been a real uplift. It's put a spring in my step that I didn't have since Monday."

I knew her husband's words gave her much strength and courage. Her last words to me at the Holmdel gathering did the same. I'll always remember them. I had just finished working eleven days straight and was exhausted. So much so that when I asked to lie down in a room backstage, just to rest for a minute before the program began, I slept for two hours! I had meant to take a 15-minute catnap, but totally zoned out. When I walked out onto the platform and saw the size of the crowd, it was just all too overwhelming. Though I speak to thousands of people every month, this wasn't about stage fright. It was about communicating what couldn't possibly be communicated. Like everyone who's spent time at Ground Zero, I knew that no matter what words I was able to find, the public really would never understand the magnitude of the destruction visited upon us September 11th. I'd just have to do the best I could.

The evening's program had Lisa Beamer speaking at 8:20 P.M. and me giving a twenty-minute message beginning at 8:53. Pregnant, the mother of two small children, this young widow found herself speaking to thousands about her heroic husband, and her faith. While I sat there listening to her, I felt increasing respect for this brave, grieving widow. When she finished speaking and sat down, I managed to tell her over the applause, "Lisa, your being here tonight has given a lot of strength and hope to these people."

She smiled warmly. "That's why I am here," she said. "I will grieve later."

AL BRACA

Al Braca worked on the 104th floor of One World Trade Center for Canter Fitzgerald, a company that lost 700 employees. Al's co-workers, who knew Al was a strong Christian, called him "the Rev." And there were times they used him as one. When the World Trade Center was bombed in 1993, it took Al's group about three hours to negotiate the stairs to safety. The story goes that as they were going down those stairs, people would ask Al for prayer. If the reports are accurate, and there's no reason to believe they're not, the same thing happened on September 11th. I never met Al; but I heard about him one night in the Family Assistance Center. I was told that a man who worked for Canter Fitzgerald called his wife on his cell phone. He told her that they all knew they were going to die and he wanted to tell her he loved her. Then he said, "Al Braca is praying with people up here on this floor." When I met Al's sixteen-year-old son, Chris, I told him the story I'd heard at the Family Assistance Center about his father. It was an honor to meet Chris, as well as Al's widow, that evening in Holmdel. Imagine your last words being prayers for all the people you work with!

When I was first introduced to Chris Braca backstage at the amphitheater I was so impressed with him. He immediately struck me as a young man of confidence and clear thought, but also someone with a gentle disposition. When I finally had a moment to speak to him, I couldn't believe he was only sixteen, he seemed so committed to his faith, so filled with God's Spirit. Toward the end of his message, Chris told the crowd about his father's sense of humor and of his integrity. He moved the arena. He moved it even more when he ended his talk by saying, "My dad was an amazing person. He taught me how to love, how to be a man of God, and he never compromised his faith."

THE POWER OF WORDS

Have you ever wondered how those close to you will remember you when you're gone? Would they say nice things, talk about how you impacted their lives in a positive way? What about your children? Would they be able to stand at the microphone in front of a large crowd and say, "My dad was an amazing person"? The rest of Chris Braca's life will be impacted positively by his dad's last words—his prayers for others that they might receive eternal life.

So you see, it's important that we choose our words well, especially our last ones. But how will we know which words will be the last we say to a person, or the last ones we say before we die? Of course, we won't. So if we don't know which will be our last words, and we want our last words to be the right ones, then we should choose *all* our words well. The Bible is packed with people who used their words to bless people, to build people up and protect them. What a blessed behavior for us to learn! James gave instruction to those in the early church about minding our words, how we should guard own tongues. Not one to use "fluffy, feel-good" words, James thought a person's life should consist of loving and serving people, not uttering religious platitudes.

> *If anyone among you thinks he is religious, and does not bridle his tongue but deceives his own heart, this one's religion is useless. Pure and undefiled religion before God and the Father is this: to visit orphans and widows in their trouble, and to keep oneself unspotted from the world.* (James 1:26-27)

For James, keeping control of the tongue is a full-time job. Easy to say, hard to do. In fact, it's so hard to do that in the next verses James compares it to taming a wild animal. But we need to do it. James goes on to describe what might happen if we don't. It's like a spark that starts a raging forest fire.

> *My brethren, let not many of you become teachers, knowing that we shall receive a stricter judgment. For we all stumble in many things. If anyone does not stumble in word, he is a perfect man, able also to bridle the whole body.*
>
> *Indeed, we put bits in horses' mouths that they may obey us, and we turn their whole body. Look also at ships: although they are so large and are driven by fierce winds, they are turned by a very small rudder wherever the pilot desires.*
>
> *Even so the tongue is a little member and boasts great things. See how great a forest a little fire kindles! And the tongue is a fire, a world of iniquity. The tongue is so set among our members that it defiles the whole body, and sets on fire the course of nature; and it is set on fire by hell.*
>
> *For every kind of beast and bird, of reptile and creature of the sea, is tamed and has been tamed by mankind. But no man can tame the tongue. It is an unruly evil, full of deadly poison. With it we bless our God and Father, and with it we curse men, who have been made in the similitude of God. Out of the same mouth proceed blessing and*

cursing. My brethren, these things ought not to be so.

Does a spring send forth fresh water and bitter from the same opening? Can a fig tree, my brethren, bear olives, or a grapevine bear figs? Thus no spring yields both salt water and fresh. (James 3:1-12)

MOVING BEYOND PAST WORDS

If you've had trouble in the past controlling your tongue, you may feel overwhelmed by the consequences. Especially, if you did something like sending your teenager off to school with some negative words only to find out later he'd been involved in an accident. Are negative last words a part of your Ground Zero? If they are, you need to know God forgives you, know that Jesus took those words with Him to the cross and atoned for them. Also know that your loved one, being your loved one, would forgive you too.

The Apostle Paul gave us a good word to live by: "Be angry, and do not sin: do not let the sun go down on your wrath" (Eph. 4:26).

What a simple truth and a simple way to end our day. Don't go to bed if you're still angry with anyone you have dealt with that day. You'll have a hard time sleeping, and when you do sleep, the anger will only be driven more deeply into your heart, making it harder to remove later. So talk it out with your mate, or call or e-mail your friend—whatever it takes to clear things up by the end of the day. And don't make excuses, just do it!

Do you know whose last words are the most "read" in history? Jesus Christ's. And he spoke them as he hung dying on a Cross. That cross was set high on Golgotha, a mound outside Jerusalem's city gates, at the intersection of the roads entering the city. His words have been read in most known languages, in most countries, in the most widely printed and circulated book ever—the Bible. Actually, Jesus spoke seven times from the cross, but we're interested in his very last words:

So when Jesus had received the sour wine, He said, "It is finished!" And bowing His head, He gave up His spirit. (John 19:30)

These three powerful words have rung out like a pealing bell through 2,000 years of history. Jesus knew His divine assignment was done. He'd come to earth, revealed the way to God, and redeemed His people, atoning for the sins of the world—my sins, your sins. His work of redemption was finished once and for all. He was the sacrifice God accepted for the sins of mankind. "It is finished" brought closure to His suffering as it should bring closure to yours as well.

Closure comes when you realize some very basic issues.

First, it's not wrong for you to move on with your life. A traumatic experience slashes deeply into our souls and often leaves us with the feeling we'll never be normal again. Not so. You will recover. And you will be stronger, more compassionate and understanding because of your experience. But there may be reasons you don't want to move on. If you're recovering from the loss of a loved one, for instance, you may feel you're being unfaithful if you move on. While others might believe that if they release the painful feelings, they're not respecting their lost loved one. Neither concept is true. Life has a lot of days in it, and God wants us to live every one of them abundantly. For someone who's lost a spouse to say "I will never remarry" creates a lot of turmoil when, a few years later, she meets someone and falls in love. For the person who's had a financial collapse to say "I will never amount to anything again" may cause a person to avoid reasonable financial risks later on, and may create a self-fulfilling prophecy if he begins to be more successful again. If the last words you spoke to the person you lost were hurtful or unloving, accept God's forgiveness. If He can forgive you and not hold this sin against you, you can ask Him to help you put all that in the past and move on.

Moving on with life is a critical part of the closure process for a painful situation. In fact, it is the sign of emotional health and mental strength to get on with life. And when you move on, do so with love and respect. If, as you begin to build your new life, you rebuild with a deep love and respect for what came before, you will always know your construction is occurring on God's foundation. Don't forget what the Bible says: "There remains therefore a rest for the people of God. For he who has entered His rest has himself also ceased from his works as God did from His" (Heb 4:9-10).

God wants you to be at peace with yourself and your circumstances. You will never be able to find closure if you continue to control your feelings and memories. This is especially true if you had harsh words or bad memories. Enter the rest that God has for you by letting go with love and respect. Remember those words that Lisa Beamer spoke when she learned of her husband's last words. She said, "It offered some emotional closure and began a new era of hope. It's been a real uplift. It's put a spring in my step that I didn't have since Monday."

May that be true of you this very day. May you gain some emotional closure and let this begin a new era of hope for you. And while you are at it, let God's Word put a spring in your step. He loves you so very much that He let His Son die on the cross for you, and His Son's last words say it all: "It is finished." Take the finished work of the cross to your heart today and rest in Jesus' finished work for you.

What a time for you to commit, that from today forward you will always be careful with your last words.

CHAPTER 17
GOD'S PERSPECTIVE

When I thought how to understand this,
It was too painful for me—
Until I went into the sanctuary of God;
Then I understood their end.

Psalm 73:16-17

THE CHURCH AT GROUND ZERO

St. Paul's is one of the oldest and most historic churches in New York City. When detective Aviles and I arrived at the church building we noticed that the police perimeter was just outside of the building. The chapel was inside the second circle of security barricades. This congregation had won the hearts of the workers. How did they do this? By making their facility into what all church buildings should be—a hospital, motel, rest stop, storehouse, and restaurant—a place of refuge from the whirlwind of activity just a block away. Firemen slept on pews, police officers and firemen knelt to pray at the altar, or sat on the floor leaning against the walls heads bowed praying and resting. Boxes of supplies for the workers were stacked in the aisles. The boxes contained gloves, hardhats, flashlights, and other stuff. In front of the facility dozens of parish members cooked hot dogs and hamburgers and passed out cold drinks.

I made my way through the sanctuary on a search for the pastor, then made my way up winding stairs to the top floor. There I paused to look out the rear window towards the tangled pile where the World Trade Center used to be. It was one of my very first personal quiet times I'd had all that day, and it was awesome. I noticed a cemetery down below to the side and back of the building. It was tightly littered with debris from the Twin Towers collapse. Seeing that debris scattered around the gray headstones, I saw like never before that death lay both underground and above ground in this old historic neighborhood. I was honored to be on this holy ground where the Gospel was not only preached and taught but being lived out by these servants who had opened their church doors.

Many churches pride themselves on how neat and tidy their grounds and facilities look. Maybe that's not a good measure. Sure we want our facilities to reflect the beauty and order of our Lord, but maybe there are times, like these times, when a facility needs to look like God has rolled up His sleeves and is doing what's needed to help. This is what He was doing at St. Paul's. And through this congregation, He gained the trust and admiration of the men in blue. Here was a sanctuary open 24/7 for the brokenhearted and weary warriors of September 11th.

TOUGH QUESTIONS

Have you ever struggled with the question of why bad people always seem to get away with murder, while you get a parking ticket when you're five minutes late getting back to the meter? Why does evil always seem to triumph and good always seem a day late and a dollar short? Good people work long and hard hours and never seem to make ends meet, while the criminals and con men get rich quick and spend their days in large hotel suites. Why does there seem to be this imbalance in the world between good and evil? Why do the wicked prosper? It just doesn't seem fair.

The writer of Psalm 73 struggled with this very same issue. Although a knowledgeable writer, his struggle reveals that many of life's questions may never be answered—not in this life here on earth, anyway. Life's unfairness, an issue debated since the beginning of mankind, certainly seems like one of them. This particular issue seems to be the reason this writer penned the psalm. And personally, I feel he's uncovered one of the great secrets of life, one that is of immeasurable help in the search for closure in an uncomfortable situation.

In most Bibles this psalm is ascribed to a man named Asaph. This is the second psalm with his name on it, and the first of eleven consecutive psalms he seems to have written. Why do I say *seems*? Scholars aren't universally convinced Asaph wrote them. Some think David wrote them and dedicated them to Asaph for singing. But in 2 Chronicles 29:30, we read that Hezekiah commanded the Levites to sing "the words of David and of Asaph, the seer." So, it is very possible that Asaph did write these words as he pondered God's deep truths. Either way, the writer is definitely wrestling with the issue at hand, the prosperity of evil men, and the pain and suffering of the godly.

Truly God is good to Israel,
To such as are pure in heart.

But as for me, my feet had almost stumbled;
My steps had nearly slipped.
For I was envious of the boastful,
When I saw the prosperity of the wicked.
(Ps. 73:1-3)

The psalmist is obviously confident in his relationship to God, confident enough to admit he almost gave up and became cynical because he couldn't understand life's inequities.

For there are no pangs in their death,
But their strength is firm.
They are not in trouble as other men,
Nor are they plagued like other men.
Therefore pride serves as their necklace;
Violence covers them like a garment.
Their eyes bulge with abundance;
They have more than heart could wish.
(Ps. 73:4-7)

The Psalmist sees that evil people never even suffer the ravages of age; even as they get old, nothing affects them negatively. As the years pile up, so do the trappings of the good life.

They scoff and speak wickedly concerning oppression;
They speak loftily.
They set their mouth against the heavens,
And their tongue walks through the earth.
(Ps. 73:8-9)

Now the writer reveals the contempt the wicked have for God and the things of God. These are the people who want to separate God from the society they live in. They curse and mock heaven and wag their heads at anything spiritual. And their tongues walk the earth proudly spreading anti-god sentiment.

Therefore his people return here,
And waters of a full cup are drained by them.
(Ps. 73:10)

The words chosen here are metaphorical, symbolic. They show us how we all feel sometimes—like we're full cups of water. But when evil people gain power they drain us and we feel empty, dry, like there's nothing of value left for us. We feel hopeless and unable to carry the good elements of our lives forward for ourselves or our society. We have no power to accomplish good because evil is in control and has sapped our strength.

And they say, "How does God know?
And is there knowledge in the Most High?"
Behold, these are the ungodly,
Who are always at ease;
They increase in riches.
(Ps. 73:11-12)

When a society rejects God, God rejects the society. God is a true gentleman and He does not push Himself upon people. He invites people to His house, and if they don't come He doesn't force them.

Like Friedrich Nietzsche, the renowned German philosopher, these people the psalmist writes about are probably the early proponents of the "God is dead" movement. Man's arrogance always hides behind intellectualism, just as Adam and Eve hid their nakedness behind fig leaves.

Years ago I saw some scribbling on the wall of a men's room, it read: *"God is Dead!" (signed) Nietzsche*. Below it and in a different handwriting was: *"Nietzsche is Dead!" (signed) God.*

A couple of years ago I was at Yale University in New Haven, Connecticut, for an afternoon rally. It was outdoors in an open plaza, and we spoke about the wonderful love God had for the student body there. Two women dressed and made up in the full black Gothic look got upset with the Gospel message and appeared a little while later with a very large sign that proclaimed in bold letters: "GOD IS DEAD." When I finished talking to the crowd, I stepped over to the young women and began a conversation with them. A smaller group of students gathered to listen. I'm from the "flower power" generation and witnessed firsthand the 1960s cultural revolution on

America's campuses. So as I talked with these "kids" I felt sorry for them. Their cause was a lost cause, but it was also one I'd supported in debates when I was their age on my campus. One of the women really didn't care much, nor did she have much to say. Her "girlfriend" was the vocal one. She was antagonistic, aggressive, and loud. After five minutes of listening to her version of "How does God know? And is there knowledge in the Most High?" I put my hand on her shoulder, leaned near her ear and whispered, "Listen, I have daughters your age and I have nothing against you, nor do I have anything to prove here. So don't embarrass yourself in front of all of these people."

This caught her off guard and the crowd was captivated. They liked that I wasn't afraid of her and that I approached her so casually and lovingly.

By that time I'd maneuvered myself in front of their GOD IS DEAD sign and blocked their message for the rest of our discussion.

Years ago I learned an axiom: "When you sling mud you are losing ground." When this antagonist saw that the crowd was laughing when I made my point humorously, or clapping when I made a particularly strong point, she began the mudslinging. I knew she was losing ground and losing it fast. When her frustration peaked, she shouted out, "God is dead! There is no God!"

I responded, "Oh no!" I actually startled her and the crowd. I leaned over again speaking into her ear, "You just quoted Scripture. I thought you didn't believe in the Bible."

Not thinking clearly, she repeated my words out loud for the whole crowd to hear. "I don't believe in the Bible! What do you mean I quoted Scripture?"

So with the door opened wide by my opponent, the Holy Spirit landed the knockout punch and the discussion was over: "Well, I responded, Psalm 14, verse 1 says: "The fool has said in his heart, 'There is no God.'"

Surely I have cleansed my heart in vain,
And washed my hands in innocence.
For all day long I have been plagued,
And chastened every morning.
If I had said, "I will speak thus,"
Behold, I would have been untrue to the generation of Your children.
(Ps. 73:13-15)

The writer's frustration is something I'm sure both you and I have felt. And the moment we feel it, we want to throw in the towel; we want to give up. "Why do I even try to do good? Every day, life just pounds on me. Why am I going through this? I try to be good, but I get nowhere." These thoughts are normal. Many times life just doesn't make sense to us. "Surely I have cleansed my heart in vain."

When your world falls apart, your mind jumps through hoop after hoop. You'll look back at the past, trying to retrace your footsteps in hopes of seeing where you made mistakes, when things began to go wrong. As you reason things out, you may challenge God; you may even challenge the concept of God. Your frustration may result in rude, unbecoming thoughts, maybe even words you later regret. Please listen carefully: closure is coming to your soul, and peace will heal your saddened heart. Trust God above all else. Remember the very first words of the psalmist: "Truly God is good." Yes, you may be frustrated, you may have suffered severe setbacks, you may be emotionally distraught. There may be no denying any of that. And the psalmist acknowledges that may be true of your situation. Remember, he tells us in verse 2 that his "steps had nearly slipped." He admits his faith wavered, that he almost surrendered to negative feelings and emotions. But God was good.

Note, he ends this section (v. 15) by saying the betterment of others is important to him. Just like Lisa Beamer said, her children would be told throughout their lives that their dad was a hero. The psalmist says that had he taken to heart the pessimistic viewpoint, had he lived and spoken the way he was thinking, he wouldn't be a faithful messenger to the people he influenced. He was searching for the high ground, and in the next two verses it's obvious he found it.

THE BEGINNING OF HEALING

When I thought how to understand this,
It was too painful for me—
(Ps. 73:16)

Thank God this verse is in the Bible! What would we do without it?

When I try to understand September 11th, I just can't force all of the pieces together. I struggle with a god named Allah who would tell his followers in his Qur'an to kill their enemies, when the God of the Bible tells

His followers to love them. I struggle with the suffering that was inflicted and pain I saw firsthand that has devastated so many lives. Although I did not suffer the pain so many others have, I was still affected. So much so that while writing this book I had to stop at least twice because tears overwhelmed me. As I formed the words, I relived the experiences they described. In writing about the rubble, I saw it again. Writing about the smells, I smelled them again. I have remembered some of the ugliest scenes of my life—the remains unearthed at "the pile," the work at the morgue. The grief I saw and heard in hundreds of family members at the Family Assistance Center became part of me again. And I've continuously revisited the gaunt, tired, yet sternly committed faces of hundreds of rescue workers—construction workers, police officers, firefighters. My heart has been wrenched over and over as mere words have made the experiences all so terribly real for me again.

Just like the psalmist, I cry out, "When I thought how to understand this, It was too painful for me."

We may never understand everything about a tragedy, and when we try to do so the thoughts are just too painful. Of course, our natural need for order makes it normal to try to understand. But when the pieces don't fit, and when the consequences cut us so deeply, there's severe emotional pain.

Remember the nursery rhyme we shared in the beginning of the book? When Humpty Dumpty fell and was shattered, all the king's horses and all the king's men could not put him back together again. The writer of Psalm 73 hasn't just thrown up his hands and said, "That's it. I give up. You figure it out. I want nothing to do with a good life or being a good person. This pain is too much for me endure, to understand." No, just the opposite: he's being emotionally honest.

Some people will turn to drugs and alcohol at this point. They feel the need to anesthetize the pain, and dulling it by just taking something for it is just the simplest alternative. Or, at least, it appears to be. We all know it's not. Or, if they don't take something for it, they push the pain away. They deny it's there, stuff it deeper down inside themselves, as far as they can get it from consciousness. If you do either of these, you'll never find closure for your Ground Zero. If you bury it, the pain will always work its way back up to the surface. If you try to anesthetize it, you'll just need more and more medication (drugs and alcohol) to make it disappear. Soon the cure will be worse than the disease. Please don't hurt yourself by taking either path.

You're on the way to closure, so just be patient, and remember: "The thoughts you are having are normal thoughts that any normal person would have in an abnormal situation." Don't lose sight of this fact: your situation is abnormal; you are normal.

Had the psalmist failed to realize this and given up, he would have never brought himself to the place described by this next statement, a place that brings us all hope. As you read this next verse let it begin a new "era" for you. With this verse we have the beginning of closure on any issue, especially one as devastating as your Ground Zero.

> *Until I went into the sanctuary of God;*
> *Then I understood their end.*
> (Ps. 73:17)

"Until" may seem like an insignificant word, but the way it's used here is profound. Here's a man writing from deep frustration and heartfelt pain, and he's being brutally honest with himself, with his audience, and, more importantly, with God. He pulls no punches. He admits he had almost lost hope in God, which caused his feet nearly to slip. He shares his firsthand experience with the powerful and influential who mock God. The pain overwhelming, his understanding thwarted, he nearly gives up. Then he enters the sanctuary of God. This is the key to the psalmist's closure.

In God's sanctuary, the psalmist received the final piece to the puzzle, actually, the only piece that mattered. And by taking possession of it, by holding it to his heart, he was able to put everything into perspective and find the peace and contentment he craved.

Every winter our family comes together for a ski week in the Rockies. Friends graciously give us their home for a few days so that we can enjoy the serenity of the snow-covered mountains. Each year we stop at Wal-Mart on the way up to buy groceries and supplies. One supply we find essential is a puzzle. I usually give up trying to do the 20-piece Donald Duck puzzle, Sandy, our daughters, and daughters-in-law get one of the 1,000-piece puzzles and make the project last for the next few days.

If one of the grandchildren accidentally knocks a piece from the table, it can be difficult to finish the puzzle. Often that one piece ends up being the puzzle's centerpiece, or it's at least key to finishing the rest of the puzzle. Until that piece is found, everything grinds to a halt. Without it, the whole puzzle loses its meaning, and the people working on it may lose perspective and an understanding of the grander scheme. But once the final piece is put in place, everything makes sense again.

The intricate mosaic of your life may have just one piece missing, and you just can't understand it all because it's too painful for you. But don't give up. You *will* recover and you *will* begin a new era for your life. God knows what's happened. He sees your world falling apart, and He isn't going to leave you or forsake you. If you draw close to Him, He promises to draw close to you. Read these words of Psalm 42 and realize that you, too, can find what you seek by going to God's sanctuary—His house.

As the deer pants for the water brooks,
So pants my soul for You, O God.
My soul thirsts for God, for the living God.
When shall I come and appear before God?
My tears have been my food day and night,
While they continually say to me,
"Where is your God?"
When I remember these things,
I pour out my soul within me.
For I used to go with the multitude;
I went with them to the house of God,
With the voice of joy and praise,
With a multitude that kept a pilgrim feast.
Why are you cast down, O my soul?
And why are you disquieted within me?
Hope in God, for I shall yet praise Him
For the help of His countenance.
(Ps. 42:1-5)

In a previous chapter we encouraged you to find a good church and make it your home of spiritual refuge. Now may we encourage you to go to God in the Spirit? Go to His sanctuary via prayer and wait there for Him. Let His Holy Spirit move within you and reveal the kingdom of God that is at hand. Yes, it is in His sanctuary that your soul will find the missing pieces to your life's puzzle. It is in God's sanctuary that your soul will find the living water to quench your emotional and spiritual thirst. He loves you so very much, and His plan is not to destroy you—His plan is to build you up and restore you. The sanctuary of God is a place of healing, a place of praise and worship, a place of joy and peace.

The Book of Revelation tells us in chapters 4 and 5 that angels surround God's throne worshiping Him. It tells us His throne room is filled with music and beautiful light, and people from every nation who have been redeemed sing and praise Him with great joy. This is the sanctuary you want to step into in the Spirit, and find the fulfillment your soul craves. Do as the psalmist says: pour out your soul and talk with God. He understands everything about you and your situation. He has the power to change your situation and bring closure to you. Though we can never go back and start all over again, we can pick ourselves up today, and from this point on begin a new era.

Enter His sanctuary, and let God put the pieces of your life in their right order. Find understanding there, and the comfort for your pain.

CHAPTER 18
SAFE HARBOR

I will say of the Lord, "He is my refuge and my fortress;
My God, in Him I will trust."

Psalm 91:2

September 11th was a horror story we pray will never be repeated. But if there is a silver lining in this blackest of clouds, it's the way this tragedy brought out the best of the American people. People from all over the United States joined together like never before to support one another. They gave money, food, supplies, emotions, and time. They also gave their encouragement and some of that came in the form of letters and packages, thousands and thousands of which were delivered every day by the US Postal Service and other delivery services to the workers at Ground Zero. Letters addressed simply to firefighters, police officers, or rescue workers were distributed in large bundles. These expressions of love from the grateful citizens of America helped refresh weary workers and give them a renewed sense of purpose for the arduous work that lay ahead of them.

FOCUSING ON THE GOOD

One sergeant told me about one group of New York police officers taking a break at the site, each with several letters and packages to open. One of them tore open a package and found a Tupperware container packed with cookies; it was from a doctor and his wife in Florida. A handwritten note was inside, thanking the workers for their courage and sacrifice. In a postscript, the wife asked, "If you can remember, and have the time, could you please send back the Tupperware?" In pencil, the doctor crossed out his wife's P.S. and wrote: "Forget the Tupperware, enjoy the cookies."

For years a debate has raged about the impact of media on society. Although some disagree, it appears the majority believe the impact of movies and television is great. Watching my little grandchildren while they watch the kid's shows and children's videos, it's obvious they're involved. Eyes glued to the tube, they laugh, dance, sing, and do just about everything the purple dinosaur and the big yellow bird tell them to do. The terrorists and spokespeople for various extremist Muslim groups call America "The Great Satan." They say we're a decadent people and our television programs pollute the world with filth. I believe much of our entertainment is vulgar, vain, and empty. But it doesn't reflect the greatness of the people of the United States.

A friend of mine owns the fifth-largest studio in Hollywood. He told me one day about a meeting he had several years ago with top movie executives. Among other issues, they discussed movies and their ratings. Someone brought up the fact that "G" rated movies often gross more than those with "R" ratings. That being true, why aren't there more "G" rated films? Isn't profit the main goal for a movie studio? Actually, the meeting revealed that "profit is not always the purpose." Oh sure, they want to make a profit, but they also want to convey a message. And in Hollywood that message seems to be more important than profit. Sometimes that message includes a big dose of filth and smut. So much of it is present in American films that those watching our films in foreign lands can easily come to believe the average American citizen approves of what these movies show.

How America reacted to September 11th largely contradicts what Hollywood has been portraying. We have seen evidence that there are many caring, generous, sympathetic, empathetic people who possess a courage of conviction that will see us through all this.

But, here's the zinger: for many in the media, "Good is not the message," and "Good doesn't always sell." Even since September 11th, there haven't been major changes in the messages we receive from television and movies. Thank God those Tupperware cookies found their way from Florida to New York, and thank God they gave all of us, the workers included, an honest insight into a married couple's home and heart. "Forget about the Tupperware, enjoy the cookies." This time, good was the message, and we all needed to hear it.

CHANGED PRIORITIES

I am not the first person who's taken this forget-the-Tupperware attitude. Today I compare everything to Ground Zero. There are issues that before might have seemed huge, but now they just don't seem to matter much. I won't waste my time with them. Compared to the collapse of these giant buildings and the loss of life, much of what I face every day has moved from the column marked "important" to the one marked "distraction." Life has new meaning for me, time has a new perspective, and the future now seems like something I want to enjoy more than work towards. When recently asked, "Did Ground Zero change your life?" I had to admit it did. As Lisa Beamer assessed it, "It began a new era."

The World Trade Center twin towers were amazing buildings and awesome to behold. For thirty years these giant buildings were the Manhattan skyline's centerpiece. At 110 stories tall, they encompassed twelve million square feet of floor space. If the 347-foot tower on top of the North Tower was included, it was the world's tallest building. There were 103 elevators carrying passengers up and down, above and below ground level. The building contained sixteen miles of staircases and had about 12,000 miles of electric cable running through it. To keep air cool, fresh, and circulating, there were 49,000 tons of air conditioning equipment installed. And on 9/11 all of it came down. Undoubtedly you've seen pictures of the pile, and I've described it in these pages—inadequately, I'm sure. But however you know what you know, you can only imagine the monumental job of clearing the crumbled remains of these towers from the site.

A million tons is 2,000,000,000 pounds. A lot of zeros, isn't it? That's approximately the amount of weight construction workers removed bit by bit, shovelful by shovelful, dump truck by dump truck, by Christmas Day, 2001. Two billion pounds is a "pile" of debris. Keep in mind that they worked 24/7 nonstop, with giant cranes hefting huge steel facades and monstrous iron girders to those incredibly large dump trucks and flatbeds lined up for blocks waiting to haul it all to Staten Island. By Christmas of 2001 about 1 million tons had been removed. Remember that. Remember also, how every little detail never leaves God's sight, including the sparrow that falls to the earth.

GOD IN THE DETAILS

Ken Childress is the chaplain for the Dinuba, California, Police Department and had volunteered to work at Ground Zero. He began working at 7 A.M. on Christmas Day, and the moment he walked through the security checkpoints he met a mother and father who were still searching for their daughter who'd been lost in the towers' collapse. Since September 11th this couple had regularly brought flowers to lay at the site. Since they were unable to get through the security checkpoints, Ken offered to take the flowers for them. At that moment, as he was talking with the couple, one of the large trucks loaded with debris roared by them. They saw something small, something insignificant, fall from the truck into the street. Ken and those with him, went over to it and picked it up. It was an employee ID badge complete with photograph that allowed the employee in quieter times to enter the Twin Towers for work. It belonged to the twenty-six-year-old daughter of these two heartbroken parents. One of the chaplains with Ken found the couple and prayed with them. Now they would be able to begin the process of closure.

What an amazing story of how God personally touched this family's life! What perfect timing, God's timing, as He brought all the elements together—Ken, the grieving couple, the truck, the badge—just the right badge of thousands of badges, just the right ounce of "debris" in over a million tons of it. What a great and personal God we serve! And these stories help bolster my faith and encourage me to continue serving Him. These stories show God is very much alive and He watches each one of us. Our best interest is His desire and, if we haven't already, we need to thank Him every day, every minute, for His love and the manifestations of it in our lives.

THE RESPITE CENTER

One of those manifestations of God's love in my time at Ground Zero was Detective Carlos Aviles. Here was a guy who worked a 12-hour shift every day as a police officer—not an easy job at all—then put in that many hours again on his time off to serve his fellow workers. That's Detective Aviles. When I arrived in New York forty-eight hours after the attack, eager to feel at least a little grounded, I called my friend Carlos. He immediately understood what I needed and made himself available to introduce me to the people I had to meet to do my job effectively, and to drive me anywhere I needed to go. On his days off he worked just as hard as he did on his regular job.

Carlos is the president of Police Officers for Christ, a Christian organization that shares benevolence with the underprivileged in the city and also provides spiritual care and encouragement to the members of NYPD. Then, late at night, when some were home sleeping, Carlos would be arranging Bibles and pamphlets on the tables at the two prayer stations he had set up at West and Liberty Streets, right in the heart of Ground Zero. This is where, after twelve- to sixteen-hour duty days, he would go to pray and encourage the workers. There were so very many things to admire about Carlos, but the one I admired most was that no matter how busy he was, he always had time to pray with the cops and the firefighters. His smile became to them like a cup of cool water in a parched land.

The Mayor's Chief of Staff called Carlos to a meeting and told him to remove his prayer tents and literature tables. Thinking the worst, Carlos was suddenly overwhelmed with concern. But then he was quickly told that the city had made provision for this comfort station to be moved to St. Joseph's Chapel, a mere 100 yards from Ground Zero. The Catholic Diocese maintained a full-time parish in the now-empty facility. NYPD Chaplain Father Romano was instrumental in making these arrangements after Father Manigan, the parish priest for St. Joseph's, was forced to move himself and his flock to a safer place. God remained, though, and now Carlos could broaden his ministry of Christ's love in an even a more centralized location.

Initially Carlos figured he could provide coffee, cake, and some chairs for the workers to sit in and rest. Ultimately, this man of faith ended up feeding hot meals and drinks to 500 workers, 24/7, for more than three months—the coldest months of the year. Close to 50,000 visits were made to that little chapel during that time. How could he afford to do it? Miraculously money poured in from individuals and churches like ours to cover the cost. What started out as two folding tables and two backyard party tents grew into a building where people could find refuge out of the elements.

The Respite Center was dubbed Safe Harbor for a couple reasons. It was just a stone's throw to the harbor, and an outreach ministry called Safe Harbor International helped significantly with the logistics. Carlos' prayer was that the center would be a place of rest for the workers at Ground Zero. But he didn't completely understand how wholeheartedly God had answered that prayer until one night he noticed several firefighters had removed their gear and boots and were walking around the center in their socks—like they might in their own homes.

Horizon Christian Fellowship in San Diego (the church I serve) sent a team of eleven every week from the day after Christmas until March to help serve at Respite. Many other churches from all over the country did the same. It wasn't long until phones were installed at the center so workers could then call home and handle business. Computers were then set up so the workers could send and receive email. In every sense of the word, it became a place of true rest and refreshment to those weary warriors.

So what does *respite* mean? Here is what my extra-large dictionary tells us: "to relieve temporarily, esp. from anything distressing or trying, give an interval of relief from." Until it was closed April 1, 2002, elements of all these units found their temporary relief: United States Coast Guard, New Jersey State Police Harbor Unit, FDNY Harbor Unit, NYPD Harbor Unit, FDNY, NYPD, Vermont Harbor Patrol, construction workers, crane operators, dump truck operators, and welders. Our church had donated a van to Police Officers for Christ and it was used to haul people, food, pastries, and drinks to and from the Respite Center. What started as a simple thought—maybe a few cops could afford to donate some coffee and cake—became full-blown meals served around the clock. I am not sure Louie Hernandez, Mayor Giuliani's Chief of Staff, expected anything this wonderful to come from his decision to move Carlos' ministry to that chapel.

But food wasn't the only nourishment served up at the Respite Center. Counseling was being done all the time, as was the sharing of experiences and the sharing of love. I've heard so many amazing stories that have come to us about the tears that were shed twenty-four hours each day at the respite of Ground Zero. From this location 10,000 Bibles were distributed; people who had never read a Bible before were now interested. And they weren't forced on anyone. They were picked up by the workers who'd often say, "Yo! Mind if I take three, for my pals?"

Father Romano had his hands full with all of the NYPD funeral services, and the family counseling that results. Plus he had his own parish he pastors in Queens. It was so magnanimous for him to open St. Joseph's for this ministry. God is going to bless him abundantly for that work, and I'm sure hundreds of workers are grateful to him for the respite they got at Safe Harbor.

It's interesting to note there is a plaque out in front of St. Joseph's dedicated to one of the first priests to shepherd the flock there. Before going to heaven he was a chaplain for the NYPD, FDNY and EMS of New York City. Years later, here is Carlos with a vision to love and serve the same people who were served by the first priest of St. Joseph's. It appears that God had prepared that facility to be a Safe Harbor since the beginning.

YOUR SAFE HARBOR

What about you and your respite? Have you found that time and that place away from the turmoil and stress? It is important that you carve out your own place you can call your own safe harbor—a place of safety and calm seas out of the storm where you can cast your anchor. After all, there's nothing wrong with waiting out the storm in peace and tranquility. And while the storm rages outside your harbor, you'll want to take this time of tranquility to spend time with God. Read your Bible and let His Holy Spirit speak to you. Just like God knew where the identification badge of a 26-year-old woman was, and just like He knew where her parents would be on Christmas Day, God knows the details of your life and your heart—and what you need that will bring closure to your situation.

Will you find your identification badge at the center of a Bible story? You just might. After all, God can speak to you any way He wants when you leave your problems for a moment and take the time to dwell on Him.

That story of the identification falling off the truck where the Chaplain stood grabs my imagination. It makes me ask some questions. What caused the piece of identification to fall from the truck? What if the crane operator had not picked the particular pile of rubble holding the badge? What if the truck had been delayed, or everyone had worked more quickly, and the truck had gotten there at a different time?

The questions keep coming. Dozens of them. And no matter how many we asked, we would begin to answer all of them the same way—God was in the details.

Elijah was God's man of the hour during one of the times when events were not going well for God's people in Israel. This time it was a famine in Israel, and God directed Elijah to the brook Cherith. Brook Cherith was a small, insignificant trickle of water that we'd have real trouble finding today. Insignificant though it may have been, God used it to refresh His servant during this desperate time of drought. God also used ravens to bring food to Elijah, since there was no food. Ravens are everywhere, and they're scavengers, unclean. Yet each morning they arrived with meat in their beaks for Elijah. God used the simple and the insignificant while at the same time, he used the supernatural.

Reading the Bible may seem like a small and insignificant element of your life when you're in anguish and turmoil and in the midst of failure. But through His Word, God can heal your broken heart and bring the closure you seek. Page by page, His love flows to you—a love that will do miracles for your soul.

As you are anchored in your safe harbor don't forget to communicate—not only with family and friends, but with God. For over thirty years, I've found that when I hold an open Bible in my hands and I place a prayer on my lips, God manifests himself in wonderful ways.

And don't feel guilty if you've already found a respite. Guilt is not from your heavenly father.

Let us therefore be diligent to enter that rest, lest anyone fall according to the same example of disobedience. For the word of God is living and powerful, and sharper than any two-edged sword, piercing even to the division of soul and spirit, and of joints and marrow, and is a discerner of the thoughts and intents of the heart. (Heb. 4:11-12)

Another safe harbor for you is among the people you love most. It's here you can speak freely, or, if you've been traumatized, it's here you can be silent. Don't isolate yourself from those you love and who love you. They can be a great source of comfort during these times. When my brother died, I knew it was awkward for the kids at high school to tell me they were sorry to hear the terrible news. They had no idea what to say, how to say it, or if they should just keep quiet. Realize this, and when you experience an uncomfortable silence, be the icebreaker. Tell them you know speaking to you at a time like this might be difficult, tell them it's okay, that you and God are together, and together the two of you will get through this. Then invite them to come along.

Posttraumatic stress is real and it can linger long after an incident. Years ago I was called by the police one evening in San Diego to talk with a suicidal man. This man threatened to kill himself, and if a cop came near he would shoot him, too. After a two-hour standoff, the police entered the home, and as they did, the man pointed his gun at them. I grabbed the man's wife and held her in my arms, covering her ears as the guns went off. It took more than nine weeks for me to get a full night's sleep after that incident. Posttraumatic stress syndrome can cripple you, sometimes in subtle ways. It can throw you off balance, push you into depression, cause you to make unwise decisions. A respite helps turn the situation around, helps you veer out of the storm, and gives you time to get away from the turmoil and begin the closure phase of your life.

If anyone knew life's stresses, it was Jesus. People surrounded Him night and day. So insistent were they for His time and attention that He had to go to mountaintops and to the center of seas to find time alone. And these weren't just a quiet bunch of groupies, either. They were crippled, leprous, sick, blind, deaf people—people in deep trouble—and they brought all those troubles, and all the stresses related to them, to Jesus. They laid them right at Jesus' feet.

> *Then the apostles gathered to Jesus and told Him all things, both what they had done and what they had taught. And He said to them, "Come aside by yourselves to a deserted place and rest a while." For there were many coming and going, and they did not even have time to eat. So they departed to a deserted place in the boat by themselves.* (Mark 6:30-32)

If anyone knew the importance of a respite, Jesus did. That's why He wants you to have a safe harbor, a place where you can rest and begin to heal.

CHAPTER 19
MOVING FORWARD

Forgetting those things which are behind and reaching for-
ward to those things which are ahead.

Philippians 3:13

As a private pilot, I learned long ago that planning for a trip was a must. If you didn't know where you were going you could get yourself into a lot of trouble. Flight planning takes some forethought and research. You must check the weather at your departure point, along the route you plan to fly, and at your final destination. It's good to look at a map and know what altitude is best to fly; there just might be some mountains in your way, or a radio tower or some other obstruction that could disrupt your plans. A preflight of the airplane is a must also, making sure you have enough fuel, checking to see that all the necessary equipment is working; checking your oil while looking for any leaks in the engine compartment. All of this will assure you that the plane is airworthy and that you should be able to fly it to your destination without problems.

But, how in the world do you ever prepare yourself for a Ground Zero? When your world falls apart how do you ever recover? In this section we're talking about closure. And when closure comes it is time to move forward with your life. This phase of any critical incident is uncomfortable at first. Much like a patient who has had hip surgery, it is those first few steps that are uncomfortable. Once the muscles get strengthened and the legs keep moving, it gradually becomes natural to walk again. So it is when calamity hits your life. There comes a time when it is good to move forward and get on with living. Give the weather station a call and find out what lies ahead; it's time to file a flight plan and move on to the next destination. God has a brand-new era waiting in your life, and closure will allow you to receive all the great and wonderful blessings that God has for you.

Blessed be the God and Father of our Lord Jesus Christ, who has
blessed us with every spiritual blessing in the heavenly places in
Christ. (Eph. 1:3)

199

DECIDING TO MOVE ON

"You watching TV?" Rick Rescorla was calling from the 44th floor of the World Trade Center, icy calm in the crisis. When Rescorla was a platoon leader in Vietnam, his men called him Hard Core, because they had never seen anyone so unflappable in the face of death.

Now he was vice president for corporate security at Morgan Stanley Dean Witter & Co., and a jet airliner had just plowed into the north tower. The voices of officialdom were crackling over the loudspeakers in the south tower, urging everyone to stay put: "Please do not leave the building. This area is secure."

Rescorla was ignoring them. "The dumb [expletives] told me not to evacuate," he said during a quick call to his best friend, Dan Hill, who had been watching the disaster unfolding on TV. "They said it's just Building One. I told them I'm getting my people the [expletive] out of here."

"Typical Rescorla," Hill recalls. "Incredible under fire."

Morgan Stanley lost only 6 of its 2,700 employees in the south tower on September 11, an isolated miracle amid the carnage. And company officials say Rescorla deserves most of the credit. He drew up an evacuation plan. He hustled his colleagues to safety. And then he evidently went back into the inferno to search for stragglers. He was the last man out of the south tower after the World Trade Center bombing in 1993, and no one seems to doubt that he would've been the last one out in September if the skyscraper hadn't collapsed on him first. One of the company's secretaries actually snapped a photo of Rescorla with his megaphone that day, a sixty-two-year-old mountain of a man coolly sacrificing his life for others.

Rick Rescorla was a man who knew where he was going. He was going down forty-four floors to safety, no matter what anyone told him. And he was so sure of his direction he helped the 2,700 other members of his company go in the right direction with him. His words "keep moving" caught my attention, because if we don't keep moving we can never have closure.

The Bible is a strong resource for you to find the strength to move forward and into the future. The apostle Paul gave us many insightful words to help make the first steps. Let's follow his steps and see if they get us headed in the right direction towards closure.

Brethren, I do not count myself to have apprehended; but one thing I do, forgetting those things which are behind and reaching for-

ward to those things which are ahead, I press toward the goal for the prize of the upward call of God in Christ Jesus. (Phil. 3:13-14)

Paul is being very humble here and letting his reader know that he is not perfect. And just because he was an apostle didn't mean he had an inside track to perfection. He knew that the Christian walk took faith and it took time. Each day of his life he would be dying more to himself and living more for his Master. Note his emphasis: "one thing I do." He is very specific, and we need to learn this lesson. He is speaking to us as an athlete, one who is running in a race. The number-one lesson in running the race of life is the same as running in a track meet. Forget the starting blocks and the yardage that is behind you—the race is before you, so run forward and run with a purpose. The term for reaching is that of grasping for something; in other words, all of his energy is devoted toward grasping for the finish line. The picture here is very vivid: the runner has an eye for nothing except that finish tape he must bust through.

One danger that befalls a victim of a critical incident is the possibility of becoming an emotional cripple. Mentally not moving beyond the incident can be extremely harmful to a person.

When I became a Christian I was twenty-six years old, and I had made a radical commitment to the commandments of Jesus Christ. There were thousands of young people like me who responded to the call of Jesus during the Jesus Movement. Four of us who lived together and had surrendered our lives to God at the same time, had met a man and woman in Santa Ana, California. They were a wonderful couple; they had been married for several years and were facing a Ground Zero of their own. The husband was a veteran of World War II, and because of being "shell shocked" he had a fear of going outside. He actually was frozen with fear and unable to let himself leave the house at all. His panic attacks were debilitating when he stepped outside the door.

The four of us went to their house every Friday night for a month, where we would have a great time talking, laughing, singing, and reading the Bible. This man was so kind and grateful for our attention and love. One night as we said our good-byes we were getting into the car and I stopped and said, "Hey, what's going on here?" We had been standing on the front lawn chatting, and then on the sidewalk until the car doors opened and we were getting in. What we did not notice was that the man and wife were both on the lawn with us and then the sidewalk. The man had actually walked outside the house with us! He didn't even realize that he had done this. Miraculously, twenty years of fear and paranoia were gone. You see, the man started moving, going in a new direction. He found the love of God so natural coming from us each week that he didn't even think of his debilitating situation. He was no longer frozen with fear because he was moving forward. From that night on we would see each other in church on Sunday, about six miles from the home that had been a place of self-imprisonment for this suffering man.

Take the advice of the apostle Paul and focus on the finish line; don't get hung up where you are right now. You don't necessarily need to beat anyone else—you just need to run your own race. The prize for crossing this finish line is an eternal prize, "the upward call of God in Christ Jesus." Using Paul's analogy of a race, focus on what is in front of you and have a goal set before you. This will allow you to begin making some forward motion in your life and that will be healthy for you.

THE UPWARD JOURNEY

Jesus spoke of that forward movement in the life of a disciple also.

> *When He had called the people to Himself, with His disciples also, He said to them, "Whoever desires to come after Me, let him deny himself, and take up his cross, and follow Me. For whoever desires to save his life will lose it, but whoever loses his life for My sake and the gospel's will save it.* (Mark 8:34-35)

I find this fascinating because of the direction Jesus was headed. He had to go up to Jerusalem because Jerusalem is set on a hill. Then he went up on the cross and then ultimately he went up to heaven. If you are going to follow Jesus you are on the up and u,p and you are on your way up. He has us moving in the right direction and it is a forward and an upward motion.

Remember the 23rd Psalm? This psalm talks a lot about moving on, doesn't it? It is the picture of a sheep that is confident in his shepherd.

> *1 The LORD is my shepherd; I shall not want.*
> *2 He makes me to lie down in green pastures; He leads me beside the still waters.*
> *3 He restores my soul; He leads me in the paths of righteousness*

For His name's sake.

4 Yea, though I walk through the valley of the shadow of death, I will fear no evil; For You are with me; Your rod and Your staff, they comfort me.

5 You prepare a table before me in the presence of my enemies; You anoint my head with oil; My cup runs over.

6 Surely goodness and mercy shall follow me All the days of my life; And I will dwell in the house of the LORD Forever.

Look at all of the movement that is taking place in this psalm of David.

Verse 2: lie down, leads me beside the still waters

Verse 3: leads me in the paths of righteousness

Verse 4: though I walk through the valley of the shadow of death

Verse 6: goodness and mercy follow and I end up in the Lord's house

This psalm is a great comfort when our world falls apart because it shows every circumstance we will confront. It is filled with a variety of promises from God. I wonder if you have ever picked out the many promises of this psalm before.

- He promises to be your provider.
- He promises to give you rest and peace.
- He promises to restore your soul.
- He promises to give you His righteousness.
- He promises you never need to fear death, or any other calamity.
- He promises to always be with you.
- He promises to anoint you with overflowing blessings.
- He promises goodness and mercy are yours forever.
- He promises you can come to His house and stay forever and ever.

If you read through the psalm again, you might find even more promises. Those are a lot of promises in one little psalm, but you can rest assured that God will fulfill his promises to you. God wants you to have the necessary faith to move forward with your life. I have learned over the years that there is much to learn on the road of life, and you learn more from your failures than you ever do from your successes. When problems outweigh the joy of living, it does not mean it is time to give up—it means it's time to let God do what He does best. He is the one to bring closure and let things begin new and fresh in your life.

I have always enjoyed Easter—above all because of the message, but also because of the time of year. Notice that God chose springtime as the perfect time for the resurrection. Spring is the time when life buds forth from the flower gardens and the orchards. New birth comes forth from the animal kingdom and the weather warms up and dissipates the snow and cold damp winter. The old world is passing away and everything new is blossoming into fruition.

We usually have at least four Easter services in San Diego—beginning on Good Friday when we meet with a few thousand people in beautiful Balboa Park, then the Sonrise Service early Easter morning at Sea World with a few thousand more people, and then back to two of our campuses for a few thousand more people. I love it because San Diego is usually bright and beautiful and sunny and warm on Easter weekend. Every year I see people from all walks of life and all ages respond to the good news that Jesus Christ has risen from the dead. Boys and girls, moms and dads, homeless people, couples—it never ends when people hear this glorious message of eternal life. Like Easter, your time of closure can be a time of new beginnings.

TAKING FIRST STEPS

What is it that you can do to get moving? Well, to begin with you need to be like a pilot and decide on your destination and begin plotting your course. Ultimately your destination should be heaven. Heaven is open for you and amazingly enough, heaven is waiting for you. All you have to do is make the decision that that is where you are headed. Then call flight service and tell them your plans, file a flight plan with them, and you are on your way. Flight Service has an 800 toll-free number, and so does heaven. Heaven is just a prayer away and it's free to call there. When you file your flight plan with flight service they put all of the pertinent data concerning your flight into their computers—aircraft make and model, number of souls on board, color of airplane, equipment on board, amount of fuel, estimated departure and arrival times, and an alternate airport in case of trouble—and you give them a telephone number so they can contact you in case you forget to cancel your flight plan on arrival. It is so much like salvation: you pray and ask God to forgive you of your sins, He empowers you to make the flight and covers all of the costs and expenses involved. Once you have made voluntary contact, heaven takes note of you and watches your life, and from here on out you are on autopilot.

Before you start to move forward it is very important to know that you are headed in the right direction and that you are on the right road. We have discussed the destination, and that is heaven. Everything from today on is going to be under the guidance of God's Holy Spirit leading and guiding you into His truth. But how do you get there? It is actually very easy to get there because you only have two roads to choose from for your journey through life. Here's what Jesus said about the options you have:

> *Enter by the narrow gate; for wide is the gate and broad is the way that leads to destruction, and there are many who go in by it. Because narrow is the gate and difficult is the way which leads to life, and there are few who find it.* (Matt. 7:13-14)

Believe it or not, one of the busiest streets in the world was pretty barren in the days immediately following the collapse of the Twin Towers. Broadway and 42nd Street has to be one of the most well-known intersections in the world. It is commonly known as Times Square. Two months after the disaster I returned to New York City to speak at a candlelight vigil at Ground Zero. My wife and our son Phillip and daughter-in-law Bethany and I went to Times Square for dinner, and it was packed again. The bright lights and the big screens make the area so exciting—like being at a party or large gathering, no matter what time of day or night—you feel the excitement in the air of the multitudes of fun-loving people. Times Square reminded me that every major city has its own version of Broadway. Smaller towns may call it Main Street; but still it is the main attraction where the action is, the street in town where it's happening.

When I thought of the words of Jesus I could see a modern analogy for His saying. Many people go down Broadway. Broadways in any area have neon signs, restaurants, theaters, hotels, movies, sporting events, and all sorts of action to attract people to the area.

That pretty much sums up the scene that Jesus was painting with His eloquent words, doesn't it? Many people go on the broad way that leads to destruction, but few people take the narrow path that leads to eternal life. Notice that the way is narrow and the gate is straight. It may not seem like much, but I have found the word study on the text of Jesus very interesting. The word that Jesus chose for *gate* is a word that is found only ten times in the Bible and it speaks of a specific gate of the larger sort. It describes one in the wall of a city or prison, temple or a palace. When used for the gates of hell it is likened to a vast prison. So being on the right path is very important in your decision to move on. Listen to King Solomon, the wisest man ever to live. He knew that the right choice was imperative:

> *There is a way which seems right to a man,*
> *But its end is the way of death.*
> (Prov. 14:12)

So you need to ask a key question: How do I know the right way? The answer comes from Jesus himself:

> *"Let not your heart be troubled; you believe in God, believe also in Me. In My Father's house are many mansions; if it were not so, I would have told you. I go to prepare a place for you. And if I go and prepare a place for you, I will come again and receive you to Myself; that where I am, there you may be also. And where I go you know, and the way you know."*
> *Thomas said to Him, "Lord, we do not know where You are going, and how can we know the way?"*
> *Jesus said to him, "I am the way, the truth, and the life. No one comes to the Father except through Me."* (John 14:1-6)

Surely you have heard the term "doubting Thomas"; this is the Thomas the term refers to. Other Scriptures also show us the doubts of Thomas, but this passage teaches us a really good lesson. When in doubt, ask Jesus.

Jesus makes it indelibly clear that He is the way to heaven and that it is through Him that we get to the Father. So to begin the journey of closure and moving forward, we need to get onto the correct path and head in the correct direction. We begin by making sure Jesus is our Lord and Savior. Lord, because that means we surrender our lives to Him and He now leads us and is responsible for us. Savior, because that means He paid the price for our sins and God will now receive us into His kingdom because He has accepted Jesus as the perfect sacrifice. So **Step 1** in moving forward with our life is to pray and receive Jesus into our hearts.

Dear God,

It is my desire to bring closure to my painful situation.

I cannot do this on my own; I need Your help.

Please come into my heart and life with Your love and mercy and grace.

I surrender to Your Son, Jesus, and ask for Him to lead me from this day forward.

Please help me take the correct steps in the right direction to heaven.

In Jesus' name I pray.

Amen.

Congratulations if you prayed that prayer and truly received Jesus into your heart. God will envelop you with His love and grace this very moment.

Step 2 is for you to get the guidebook into your hands that will show you the direction to heaven. We have mentioned it before throughout this book: it is the Bible. Begin reading the Bible every day. Find a translation that you are comfortable with and that makes reading enjoyable. If for whatever reason you are unable to buy one at your local bookstore or Christian Bible bookstore, try to pick one up at a local church, or contact us at www.horizonsd.org and we will send you one free of charge. I would suggest starting in the New Testament with the Gospels—Matthew, Mark, Luke, and John; they tell you about His life and His love for you. The epistles are letters to Christians from the founding fathers of the church. They are basic Christian living instructions. Just read as much as you can every day and try to memorize verses that speak to your heart. You will hear the Holy Spirit speaking to you the truths of God as you read the printed page.

Step 3 is just as easy as the first two steps: Prayer is a must for you to survive anywhere on planet Earth. Prayer keeps you in contact with headquarters. It is like the pilot speaking to ground control at a busy airport. Ground control is up in the tower and they can see you and all of the other airplanes on the airport. The ground controller can safely guide you to your final parking place. Prayer is like the tower controller who gives the pilot permission to take off and to land; he knows the flow of all the traffic in and around a five-mile radius of the airport, and he can guide you safely out of the traffic pattern or safely into the traffic pattern. Use prayer as a communication channel between you and God. He is there 24/7 for you and will always respond. The Bible says, "Pray unceasingly." Prayer is not something that religious people do; prayer is conversation between you and God. It is you speaking your heart and mind openly and sharing with God, and another part of prayer is listening. So be prepared to hear from God when He hears from you.

Step 4 is an important step for you to continue on in strength. Find a church that teaches the Bible and is filled with loving people who are following God by faith. Jesus said, "you will know them by their fruit." Love is the fruit of the Holy Spirit, and it is the badge of the Christian. You don't need a cult or some exclusive sect to join. Just find a church home where you feel comfortable and where you can see the love of Jesus in the people around you.

Be sure it is a church that teaches the Bible and encourages you to grow in the knowledge of God.

Step 5 may seem hard but it's not. After all, you have already taken four steps and you are moving forward. Begin telling other people about Jesus and the difference He has made in your life. We call it witnessing to someone. All you are doing is being a witness for Jesus in your circle of influence. Don't be ashamed to talk about God and let people know that you love Him. He is not ashamed to identify with you, and He will give you the power to be His witness.

This afternoon as I was writing, our youngest daughter called to talk with Sandy. I had answered the phone and asked how she was doing. I could hear our grandson in the background and asked how he was doing. His other grandparents had just purchased him a small replica of a regular old-fashioned bicycle. He is three years old, so you can imagine the size. He has been riding his three-wheel tricycle for a while, so this is a whole new world for him to enter into. I asked if it had training wheels on the back, and she answered yes. Megan and Parker were together on the sidewalk in front of their home, and she had called on her cell phone. Megan said, "And it has a bell on it too"—at which Parker began ringing his little bell to his heart's content. What more could a three year old ask for on a sunny Saturday afternoon—his mother beside him, his Boppa on the phone, his first two-wheel bicycle (with training wheels), and his very own bell to ring all day long?

It won't be long until the training wheels are off, then it will be on to a "big boys" bike, then the teenage years and an off-road bike—and on and on goes the parade of life.

When you're taking these first steps, you might feel like your bike needs training wheels. That's OK. Don't be afraid, your training wheels will compensate during these early steps, until the day you are ready to take them off and ride like the wind.

CHAPTER 20
BEGIN TO REJOICE

A merry heart does good, like a medicine,
But a broken spirit dries the bones.

Proverbs 17:22

Someone once said, "I'd rather see a sermon than hear one." This, of course, is speaking of living the truth and being an example of the truth. The world would not have one ounce of hope if Jesus had not done just this. His entire thirty-three years that were lived on this earth were years of example. Yes, He preached and He taught, but when you study His life closely it is easy to recognize that He led an exemplary life. His friend and disciple John wrote, "And there are also many other things that Jesus did, which if they were written one by one, I suppose that even the world itself could not contain the books that would be written" (John 21:25).

JESUS' EXAMPLE

Jesus actually did something we find hard to see in our modern lifestyles: He "walked the talk." In fact, had Jesus not lived what He preached, His following would be nothing today. Thousands of hospitals, schools, orphanages, clinics, rehab centers that have been built in His name would not be around today.

Think of Franklin Graham's ministry, Samaritan's Purse. This wonderful organization of dedicated people has built hospitals in many countries. When there is a major disaster or outbreak of war, Samaritan's Purse has millions of dollars worth of relief goods immediately shipped to the area. The great thing is that Samaritan's Purse doesn't just send food, clothing, and medicine. They send doctors to administer that medicine, and volunteers to cook and distribute that food and help dispense the clothing. It is not uncommon to see dozens of volunteer construction workers putting up tent cities or building a clinic for the poor and needy. And Franklin is there right at the front of the volunteers, leading them into the situation and observing firsthand what needs to be done and who he has to connect with to get the adequate help the suffering people need.

Why has this man dedicated himself to serving the suffering of the world? Why do his wife, Jane, and their children allow this head of their household to give so much of himself to a dying world? It is an easy question for me to answer today—because Franklin is serving Jesus Christ, Jane is serving Jesus Christ, and their children are serving Jesus Christ. And when you think of it, Samaritan's Purse is only one organization that does its work in the name of Jesus Christ; there are thousands more around the globe. Where would this world be today if the love for Jesus were not in it? It is the love of Jesus, shown by His people throughout the centuries, that has kept some sanity in the troubled areas of this planet.

You see, if Jesus had only preached good sermons and taught spiritual platitudes to the masses, He would have been just another good man, another guru for the spiritually inclined. He would never have been accepted as God's Son, and we would not have confidence that His death has paid the ransom for the sins of mankind. If He had never come out of the tomb to show the world that there is resurrection power, we would all be walking with our heads down every day of our lives. Since He did rise from the dead and He did come out of the tomb, we all have tremendous hope today for our lives and for the future.

THE KEY TO CLOSURE

Here is Matthew's description of the first words spoken by Jesus after He rose from the dead:

Now after the Sabbath, as the first day of the week began to dawn, Mary Magdalene and the other Mary came to see the tomb. And behold, there was a great earthquake; for an angel of the Lord descended from heaven, and came and rolled back the stone from the door, and sat on it. His countenance was like lightning, and his clothing as white as snow. And the guards shook for fear of him, and became like dead men.

But the angel answered and said to the women, "Do not be afraid, for I know that you seek Jesus who was crucified. He is not here; for He is risen, as He said. Come, see the place where the Lord lay. And go quickly and tell His disciples that He is risen from the dead, and indeed He is going before you into Galilee; there you will see Him. Behold, I have told you."

BEGIN TO REJOICE

So they departed quickly from the tomb with fear and great joy, and ran to bring His disciples word.

And as they went to tell His disciples, behold, Jesus met them, saying, "Rejoice!" And they came and held Him by the feet and worshiped Him. (Matt. 28:1-9)

The word "rejoice" is the most reassuring of words that we could hope to hear from a man who had just conquered death. The Greek word *chairo* was used at the beginning of letters to give one a greeting. This word is used seventy-four times in the Bible, and fourteen of those times it was chosen to simply mean "be glad"; in forty-two other instances it was used to mean "rejoice." BINGO! We have found the answer to complete closure from our pain and suffering—Rejoice and be glad! Wow!

I am so happy that Jesus didn't come from the tomb and say to the women there, "Wow, that is one scary event," or "the grave is so cold and dark I was really frightened" or "I just don't know what to say, I am so shook from my experience with death." No, not at all—He did not even dwell on the subject of death or the act of dying or the pain and suffering that accompanied His crucifixion. Instead He gave us all the hope we will ever need to move forward in our lives and towards our goal of reaching heaven in His name: "Rejoice, be glad!"

The Bible says that death is something that everyone has feared, and we all have been held in bondage by this fear. In Hebrews 2:15 we read that one of the things Jesus came to Earth to do was "release those who through fear of death were all their lifetime subject to bondage."

Remember that in the storm Jesus said, "Don't be afraid," and in the garden He said, "Be glad and rejoice." These words are very important for us to hear because they allow us to move forward with the right foundation. The foundation of God's Word is going to allow you to continue your journey towards heaven along that narrow path that few people are on. Psalm 119:105 says, "Your word *is* a lamp to my feet and a light to my path."

The Bible is God's Word, and it will become the lamp for your feet and shed the necessary light upon the path you are walking. Go forward night and day and let the truth of the Scriptures guide you at all times, in all weather, under all circumstances, in every situation.

Take strength, for instance, from the apostle Paul's teaching about death in his letter to the Corinthians:

The last enemy that will be destroyed is death. . . . So when this corruptible has put on incorruption, and this mortal has put on immortality, then shall be brought to pass the saying that is written: "Death is swallowed up in victory."
   O death, where is your sting?
   O Hades, where is your victory?
   (1 Cor. 15:26, 54-55)

Now read the words of Jesus, years after His resurrection when He appeared to the apostle John on the Isle of Patmos: "I am He who lives, and was dead, and behold, I am alive forevermore. Amen. And I have the keys of Hades and of Death" (Rev. 1:18).

Yes, Jesus has the keys to hell and death and there is nothing for you to ever fear again. Hopefully you now understand why Jesus could easily tell the women in the garden that first Easter morning, "Be glad and rejoice!" With Him in your heart you will never have to have an apprehension concerning death or experience fear again. "For God has not given us a spirit of fear, but of power and of love and of a sound mind" (2 Tim. 1:7).

HEALING JOY

Closure is very important when we have received a jolt to our lives such as a Ground Zero experience. You may view the situation as completely negative, and rightfully so in most cases. However, with a little scriptural insight you can see that the spirit of joy is not only acceptable—joy has tremendous healing powers which come with it. Solomon said it very clearly in the proverb we quoted at the beginning of this chapter: "A merry heart does good, like medicine, but a broken spirit dries the bones."

When my older brother died, he left a beautiful twenty-one-year-old wife and a one-year-old son, Chris. This boy is a full-grown man with his own family now and has become very successful. Though his mother and my mother have not seen much of each other since she remarried many years ago, they have kept in touch. My nephew has been very kind to my mother, and ever since he was a little boy the two of them have had contact. But in the past few years my mother has been saddened—as any grandmother would—because his calls had quit coming. She felt especially sad about this because he is the only child of her oldest son. She had a broken spirit in this area of her life, and just like the Scripture says, it gave her dry bones.

Chris just called me out of the blue while I was writing this chapter. Starting the phone call out as the "Prodigal Nephew," he graciously apologized for not staying in touch and told me the reasons why. He had not felt like much in recent years because he had gone through a divorce and felt he had let down his family and others who were close to him. His half-brother, Kevin, was very musical, was very close with Cheryl Crow, and had produced her first hit album and sung with her on a couple of the songs that he wrote for her. Kevin had died during the time of Chris's divorce, and these two back-to-back Ground Zeros knocked him for a loop. Tonight after our hour-and-twenty-minute telephone call, he called my mother. I know that her dry bones will fill with joy and peace will flood her heart when she hears his voice.

This only happened minutes ago as I was coming to this section of writing, and I use it as an analogy for you. When you begin moving forward and closure begins, don't forget the people who love you, don't forget those near you and around you. You can have a tremendous effect by bringing joy to the hearts of others, and that joy will overflow into those dry bones of yours and theirs. Taking your eyes off of yourself is a must for closure to take place; and putting your eyes on others will allow you to be occupied with something other than your Ground Zero.

Though some people believe that Mary only had Jesus and that she remained a virgin all of her life, the Bible tells us that Joseph and Mary had several children after Jesus was born in Bethlehem.

And when He had come to His own country, He taught them in their synagogue, so that they were astonished and said, "Where did this Man get this wisdom and these mighty works? Is this not the carpenter's son? Is not His mother called Mary? And His brothers James, Joses, Simon, and Judas? And His sisters, are they not all with us? Where then did this Man get all these things?" (Matt. 13:54-56)

We see the names of four brothers, and the word *sisters* being plural means there were at least two girls, which means there were at least six children other than Jesus in Joseph and Mary's household. It was Jesus' brother James who wrote the Book of James in the New Testament. Here are some of his challenging words:

My brethren, count it all joy when you fall into various trials, knowing that the testing of your faith produces patience. But let patience have its perfect work, that you may be perfect and complete, wanting nothing. (James 1:2-4)

The reason I call these challenging words is because it is so contrary to our human nature to rejoice in rough and tough times. If you can grasp this truth, just as the athlete the apostle Paul spoke of grasps for the tape at the finish line, you are on the way to a complete and gentle closure from the struggles you have faced.

If you will follow with me as we look at the words of James, I think the theme of joy and rejoicing will become very clear to you. How in the world could James say that people should count it all joy when they fall into trials? The key here is the word in the original language that is translated "trials." The word doesn't refer to meaningless hardships or difficulties, but testing that is directed toward an end. The idea is that the person who is tested will be stronger as a result of the testing.

JOY IN SPITE OF TRIALS

The point is that you can and should begin to rejoice knowing that death is destroyed by Jesus, and that all you have faced will ultimately make you a stronger, better, and more loving person in the future. We may never know nor understand the "whys" of God. We don't know why He allows certain things to happen to us. So many people at Ground Zero have expressed their anger at God. They've asked the inevitable question, "How could God allow this to happen?" They forget to look at the obvious: "How could the devil be so evil to do such a thing as this?"

We do know this fact: 9/11 was not God's work. It was the work of those without love.

Beloved, let us love one another, for love is of God; and everyone who loves is born of God and knows God.

He who does not love does not know God, for God is love.

In this the love of God was manifested toward us, that God has sent His only begotten Son into the world, that we might live through Him.

In this is love, not that we loved God, but that He loved us and sent His Son to be the propitiation for our sins.

Beloved, if God so loved us, we also ought to love one another.
(1 John 4:7-11)

This Bible passage does reveal to us who was piloting the planes that crashed September 11th into the rural field in Pennsylvania, the Pentagon in Washington D.C., and the World Trade Center in New York City. It was hatred. If hatred flew those planes as missiles of destruction, we can be assured from the Bible that it was not God that instigated those plans. Even though the terrorists claim they did it for the glory of God, the Bible says differently. It says that God is love—not hatred and anger full of vengeance or political purpose. A person who knows God, as John tells us, is a person of love, not destruction.

In reading the New Testament it becomes obvious that Peter stands out from the crowd. He seems to be very charismatic, and a true character in every sense of the word. There is a progression in the spiritual growth of Peter that can be followed carefully. From the time when Jesus called him to serve Him and follow Him, until the time Peter himself was crucified, he was "on the move" towards maturity. He moved from being a man who had an answer for everything to become a man who relaxed his grip on life and trusted that God had all the answers.

In this you greatly rejoice, though now for a little while, if need be, you have been grieved by various trials, that the genuineness of your faith, being much more precious than gold that perishes, though it is tested by fire, may be found to praise, honor, and glory at the revelation of Jesus Christ. (1 Peter 1:6-7)

Joining the thought of James, Peter explains that there is purpose to our struggles in life. He not only relays the message to us that trials and tribulations are various in nature and they can cause grief, he reminds us that our faith is extremely valuable. It is this value that is put upon faith that captures our attention. We are told that our faith is much more precious than gold. Just like James, Peter says that we can "greatly rejoice" during the times we have struggles, pain, and suffering. When Peter made the remark "now for a little while" he was very faithful to remind us that our lives will return to normal, that closure will eventually come for our trials and tribulations.

Finally, there is much healing in the words of Paul to the Roman church for us today as well:

Therefore, having been justified by faith, we have peace with God through our Lord Jesus Christ, through whom also we have access by faith into this grace in which we stand, and rejoice in hope of the glory of God. And not only that, but we also glory in tribulations, knowing that tribulation produces perseverance; and perseverance, character; and character, hope. Now hope does not disappoint, because the love of God has been poured out in our hearts by the Holy Spirit who was given to us. (Rom. 5:1-5)

How healing and helpful these words are to us today, and just as relevant as they were to the people living in Rome under the persecution of Caesar during the first century. "Justified" by faith means "just-as-if-I'd-never sinned." It takes faith to receive the justification. And note that peace comes to our lives when we settle the ultimate Ground Zero of all—that is, our destiny for all of eternity. When we speak about our worlds falling apart, our eternal destiny is the ultimate issue for each of our lives.

This text has four tremendous points for us to remember:

First, we have peace with God.

Second, we rejoice in hope.

Third, we rejoice in tribulations.

Fourth, we are given a sequence of healing and closure that show us our faith truly is much more precious than gold: perseverance, character, hope.

All three of these personal traits are brought to us through our Ground Zero experiences. Please notice that "hope makes us not ashamed." Though we cannot understand all that comes our way through our lives, we can see the divine handwriting on the walls of our hearts, telling us, "Be of good cheer, don't be afraid," "be glad and rejoice."

In closing may I say that it is my prayer that somehow God Almighty can use this simple book to speak to your heart and strengthen your soul. He knows I am not a writer and that I feel very inadequate in attempting to write this book. He also knows that this has been a difficult endeavor for me because of the difficult situations I have had to revisit while writing. But above all He knows how much you need His tender touch and gentle words to bring you to a better place in life. God loves you, He has always loved you, and He will always love you. There really is nothing you can do to earn

His love because it is a free gift from Him to you. But take it from one weary traveler to another: God will take the shock of your collapsing world upon His shoulders. God will rescue you in your time of need. God will help you recover from your Ground Zero, and God will bring emotional closure and help you "begin a new era."

Remember these words of Jesus (John 16:33):

These things I have spoken to you, that in Me you might have peace. In the world you will have tribulation; but be of good cheer, I have overcome the world.